Daylilies-
A Fifty-Year Affair

Daylilies–
A Fifty-Year Affair

The Story of a Society and Its Flower

Frances Gatlin

drawings by H. Stephen Baldwin

PUBLICATION OF THE AMERICAN HEMEROCALLIS SOCIETY

EDGERTON, MISSOURI, 1995

Library of Congress Cataloging-in-Publication Data

Gatlin, Frances.
   Daylilies—a fifty-year-affair : the story of a society and its
flower / Frances Gatlin ; drawings by H. Stephen Baldwin. — 1st ed.
     p.   cm.
   Includes bibliographical references.
   ISBN 0-9631072-1-6 (hardcover)
   1. American Hemerocallis Society—History. 2. Daylilies.
I. American Hemerocallis Society. II. Title.
SB413.D3A445   1995
635.9' 34324—dc20   95-36874
                                               CIP

Previously copyrighted material "Hem-antics" published with permission of the artist
Printed in the United States of America
Printed on acid-free paper

CONTENTS

Foreword

WITH THIS PUBLICATION, the American Hemerocallis Society celebrates its golden anniversary. *Daylilies—A Fifty-Year Affair* captures the essence of the development of the organization, its people, and the daylily.

In 1946, the Midwest Hemerocallis Society was created in answer to Helen Field Fischer's call to have a "get together," a flower show, and a brown bag picnic at Henry Field's Nursery in Iowa. From these humble beginnings has come a society of more than nine thousand members. Under its new name, The American Hemerocallis Society, it has become international in scope, complex in nature, and the sole registrar of the genus *Hemerocallis*.

Recently, as my wife and I had the occasion to make daily trips across the grounds of a new hospital, we noticed a group of landscapers adding a mixture of sand and pine bark to long, unplanted beds. Another group busied itself preparing other planting sites for shrubs and perennials. Eventually, all beds were planted except for the long bed at the entrance to the hospital. When a final truck arrived with its quota of plants, we were surprised and pleased to see that it held a load of daylilies. As big clumps of our favorite plant were thrown from the truck, one planter asked, "What are these?" "They're daylilies," another answered, "and they make pretty flowers every year."

Only a few years ago, this incident could not have taken place. Today, however, the daylily has come to the fore as a choice landscape plant which is a reliable, good-blooming perennial capable of holding its own in almost any landscape setting.

There is no doubt that the earliest hybridizing pioneers, such as Yeld, Perry, Stout, Kraus, and others, had their share of problems. Foremost, the daylily plants used in the hybridizing work were scarce and either too tall or mostly shades of yellow or orange. The aim of these pioneers was simple—to produce hybrid daylilies in any other color but yellow or orange. One of their first breaks came with the production of a "pink" of sorts. Although it was not nearly a clear color by today's standards, it did represent a great leap forward in hybridizing away from the yellow-orange rut. Here was the beginning for many hybridizers' journeys toward what we know as the daylily of today.

Through the ensuing years, hundreds of hybridizers have made the daylily big and fat, skinny and long, tiny and round, flat and fluffy, wavy and fringed, and everything in between. Most of the known colors are here except for the purest whites and the truest of blues, which are eagerly being considered in many hybridizing programs. We remain closer to white than to the truly blue daylily that is yet a hopeful dream. In contrast, the 1949 *Yearbook* quotes a very confident Dr. E. J. Kraus stating that "the blue is not far off. I now have two seedlings which are a bright blue purple. It remains to eliminate the red from these blue purples and leave the blue."

As we reflect, through this book, on the changes that have occurred in both the daylily and our society, and as we ponder changes still to come, we should remember that it has been just fifty years since Shenandoah, Iowa. The germ of an idea proposed by Helen Field Fischer inspired the planting of seeds of enthusiasm and much more. The results have become the grand organization that continues to grow today—The American Hemerocallis Society.

Clarence J. Crochet

—CLARENCE J. CROCHET, *Past President*
American Hemerocallis Society, 1978-1979

Acknowledgments

ISTORY IS SHAPED by the individuals who live it. No less so is the telling. This book could not have been produced without voices from the past that speak through the pages of fifty years of AHS publications. We are indebted to members who donated *Journals* to form a complete set for reference. Many friends and members contributed materials, services, and encouragement—all without compensation. Special thanks are due to

- The Regional Vice Presidents who first suggested the anniversary publication.
- Publication Committee members Curtis High (chairman), Jim Brennan, Earlene Garber, Martha Seaman, and Van Sellers, who performed specific assignments, as well as members of the board of directors who supported the project.
- "Literary Consultants" Earlene Garber, Don Marvin, and Martha Seaman, who critiqued chapters in progress.
- Clarence Crochet who checked the manuscript for historical accuracy, Van Sellers who reviewed Chapter 5, and individual board chairmen who checked specific chapters applicable to their committees.
- Curtis High who proofed the copy.
- Charter members who contributed reminiscences for Chapter 1.
- Jim Brennan, who reviewed the author's material for Chapter 7, and, with the Scientific Studies Committee and the Species/Scientific Robin, supplied a bibliography of scientific material.
- The hybridizers who supported color in Chapter 8.
- Harvey Horne, AHS Slide Chairman, who coordinated and evaluated the slides for Chapter 8.
- Member-artist Steve Baldwin who gave permission to use his "Hem-antics" and supplied the daylily line drawings for chapter-opening pages.
- Patricia Crooks Henley who researched and reported the origin of the term *daylily* as a single word (page 116).
- Typographer Judith Sutcliffe (not a member) who created a set of decorative initial caps for the book. The typeface will be marketed under the name "DAYLILIES." Although Judith now lives in Santa Barbara, California, she is a native of Audubon, Iowa, not far from our Shenandoah roots.
- Those who supplied historical material and information: Bob Brooks, Bertie Ferris, Larry Harder, Betty Hudson, Eugene Latimer, Clarence Mahan, Don Marvin, Steve Moldovan, Sanford Roberts, Shenandoah Historical Society, Stanley Saxton, and Carole Skinner.
- All those who supplied slides and pictures. Special thanks to Oscie Whatley, who made two trips to the Missouri Botanical Gardens to photograph Stout Medal winners. Slide Chairman Harvey Horne contributed many slides and prints from his own collection. Sydney Eddison graciously lent slides collected for her own book, and Larry Harder delved into his historical files for hard-to-find slides and prints of some of our very early members. Others who sent slides and photos of people or daylilies were Linda Sue Barnes, Geraldine Couturier, Nell Crandall, Clarence Crochet, Mary Gage, Joiner family, Bill & Betty Munson, and Tom Wise.
- Neil Gatlin who assisted with production, all the while enduring neglect, clutter, and fast food as this book came to life.

The above list is woefully incomplete. We are grateful to all who participated in the recording of our fifty-year affair with daylilies.—F. G.

Introduction

THE PASSAGE OF FIFTY YEARS is but the blink of an eye in the history of the *Hemerocallis* and its christening by Linnaeus more than two centuries ago. Even "modern" daylily hybrids predate the American Hemerocallis Society. So it is not the daylily's birthday we celebrate, but that of a Society dedicated to "promotion, development, and improvement of the genus *Hemerocallis*." And with all due reverence to the continuity of that plant, it has never been the same since 556 single-minded gardeners converged on the small town of Shenandoah, Iowa, just fifty years ago.

This book is concerned with the period from 1946 to 1996. The events are not always chronologically arranged, and there are holes, hopefully not in the sense of inaccuracies, although that, too, is possible. These are stories as the members have seen and lived them, stories that are colored by the angle of a hundred different lenses. It is through a composite view that the broad picture emerges.

At this writing, the AHS claims upwards of 9,500 members. Each is vital to the fabric of the Society. Selecting a sampling for this book was akin to the agony of picking ten favorite daylilies. The AHS Awards & Honors inspired choices in two cases: (a) hybridizers who have been honored with the annual Bertrand Farr Award, and (b) daylilies that have received the Stout Silver Medal. Both categories are given extensive coverage. For the first time, color photographs of all the Stout Medal winners are published as a group. This chronological record of each year's top cultivar award is an indicator of progress and direction in daylilies since 1950.

The hybridizers have cooperated in an effort to show a collection of work that is being done today. No one can accurately read the crystal ball, but it is fun to try.

The evolution of important functions of the Society are covered in some detail: cultivar registration, publications, and Awards & Honors. The scientific research performed by the Society could not be adequately summarized in these pages, but two bibliographies offer references to studies done in and outside the Society. If all this seems a bit on the serious side, artist Steve Baldwin is standing by at the end with a different point of view.

Most of all, this book is a celebration. As we look back on fifty years as an organization, we hope these pages will awaken pleasant memories for those who have lived them. New growers may well be grateful for accomplishments already in place. Still others will see that the story is neither finished nor entirely rosy. Some goals remain just out of reach and a few gremlins continue to dance on the edge of our complacency. There are enough new challenges to keep us busy for another fifty years.

Meanwhile, let us pause to savor a past that is already directing the future.

Happy anniversary, AHS!

Chapter 1

Once Upon a Time

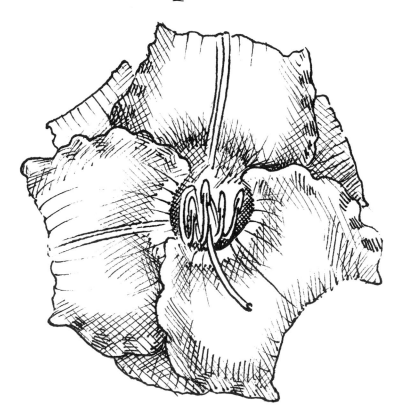

In ancient Greece they called it Aspodel,
Till Theophrastus, the first to write of plants,
Observing how this simple wayside flower
Drew from the barren soil its scanty dole
And gave each bud one day of loveliness
Of fragrance, color, symmetry and grace,
Suggested to his world the better name
Of Hemerocallis, Beautiful for a Day,
And wise Linnaeus chose the better name.
HELEN FIELD FISCHER

A Place Called Shenandoah

HENANDOAH, IOWA—population 6,000 in 1924 and about the same today. Nestled in the Nishnabotna River Valley, amidst the gently contoured plains of southwest Iowa, it seems an unlikely place to have played mother-host to the formation of an international horticultural society. Yet the Shenandoah citizenry was then, and still is, close to the earth.

The town received its name in 1870 from Civil War veterans who thought it resembled the Shenandoah Valley in Virginia. The native black soil, called loess, is rich. Corn and cattle thrive.

When our story begins in 1946, two things set this town apart—

* *Its seedhouses:* Namely, Earl May Seed & Nursery Company and Henry Field Seed Company.
* *Its radio stations:* KMA and KFNF, again, Earl May's and Henry Field's.

To say that these two enterprises were friendly competitors is to understate the case; but for our purposes, we will look more closely at Henry Field's.

The Shenandoah radio stations date back to 1924, when Henry Field's 500-watt "Friendly Farmer

1-1. Henry Field, founder of the nursery that bears his name and of radio station KFNF that began on the third floor of the seedhouse. Eventually, a small detached building was added next door from which Helen Field Fischer conducted her broadcasts.

Before all was said and done, the Field complex in downtown Shenandoah included everything from an auditorium to a tourist court. Built in a popular style of Spanish architecture, it was an early twentieth-century version of the shopping mall. The original building was gutted by fire in 1994, but the stucco walls survived intact to recall the charm of a bygone day.

Henry Field was an innovator but not the businessman that his competitor was. By 1945, he had lost control of the seed company. He died in 1949 at the age of 78, remembered as a strong family man of high moral character.

The American Hemerocallis Society is indebted to the large Field family for hosting the first daylily meeting and for contributing several key members, including Henry's sister Helen Field Fischer.

Station" began broadcasting songs by the Seedhouse Girls and the Cornfield Canaries. More to the point were discussions of subjects like "Flowers and Their Influence on the Home." (In the early part of the century, proficiency in Domestic Science—by the housewife, of course—was an assumed requisite to a happy marriage.)

The importance of radio in the early part of the twentieth century could hardly be underestimated. Farms were isolated and television existed only in the imagination of H.G. Wells. The Shenandoah radio stations in particular were a phenomenon of their day, made so by the larger-than-life personalities of their owners.

Earl May was the P.T. Barnum of the garden trade while Henry Field was the horticulturist and visionary. It was Henry Field who first saw the advantage of utilizing the power of radio to expand his seedhouse trade. Earl May, master of one-upmanship, quickly followed suit. In this small town the two seedsmen provided increasingly elaborate live entertainment staged in rival auditoriums. Both radio stations boosted their wattages until by 1940 each claimed to have been intercepted on foreign shores, although the message must have been scratchy indeed.

Each station employed popular hosts who aired programs on cooking, homemaking, and gardening. The positions were usually filled by local women, possessed of an easy manner and articulate down-

photo courtesy of Sydney Eddison

1-2. Helen Field Fischer, author, radio home-maker, hostess to the first daylily meeting in Shenandoah. Winner of the AHS's first Helen Field Fischer Award. Sister of Henry Field.

home style that captivated listeners as far away as California—on a good day. These broadcasters were unpretentious practitioners of a specialized trade known as "radio homemaking."

Such was the role filled by the Flower Lady, Helen Field Fischer.

Meanwhile . . .

The Round Robin Party

HE YEAR 1946 was a factor in our story. World War II had finally come to a close. Four years of deprivation, rationing, and restrictions were winding down. The radio stations resumed their normal programming which included Helen Field Fischer's "Garden Club of the Air." Politically correct Victory Gardens (all veggies) that had prevailed throughout the war years again made room for flowers.

The radio stations claimed among their listeners several Round Robin correspondents. Some of these

were organized by Helen Field Fischer herself while others were under the wing of a popular gardening magazine, *Flower Grower.* Remembering the great pre-war flower shows, Robin members longed for such a party. Enthusiastic plans developed along the circuit. The event would be held in Shenandoah, at the invitation of Mrs. Fischer, radio friend and mentor to scores of corresponding gardeners.

Ten years later, the 1956 Round Robin Chairman, Viola Richards, would describe the events leading up to the meeting and the formation of the

Midwest Hemerocallis Society. Her firsthand account follows:

"IN THE BEGINNING"

That the Round Robins played an important role in the formation and growth of our Society may not be known by some of our newer members.

For several years *Flower Grower* magazine had a Round Robin Department in the charge of Marion Thomas. Groups were formed on diverse subjects, with their members scattered all over the United States. The first Hemerocallis Round Robin was formed in 1943 under the leadership of Mrs. Charles Hindman, then of Overland, Missouri, but now a resident of Sebring, Florida. I became a member of the group and later took charge of it and some of the newly formed groups. Mary Claytor, St. Joseph, Missouri, became a member of one such group and through her I learned that Round Robins were circulating in the Midwest. They received their impetus from the Flower Lady, Helen Field Fischer, whose daily half-hour programs over KFNF, of the Henry Field Seed Company, Shenandoah, Iowa, were eagerly followed by flower lovers in Iowa, Nebraska, Kansas, and Missouri.

Since Mrs. Fischer could not personally answer all the letters, she suggested the formation of Round Robins by those interested in the same things. Daisy Ferrick took charge of one for daylilies. Mrs. Claytor was one of its members as was Marie Anderson, who later took charge of other groups. I became a member of that first group and through it met Mrs. Fischer.

For many years the Henry Field Seed Company had sponsored a Flower Show but during World War II it had been discontinued. In a Robin letter after the war Mrs. Anderson suggested that the shows be resumed, so Mrs. Fischer agreed to see what could be done about it. When the next "flight" of letters returned, plans were in the making for a show and the writers said, "Viola, you must come." This I dismissed as desirable but impossible, but pressure finally became too strong to resist, so I went. I knew no one except through correspondence but identification was all that was needed to put one on an old-friend basis.

There was a strong feeling that there should be an organization to provide information on daylilies and during that Flower Show the time seemed to have arrived. Mrs. Fischer promoted both daylilies and the Show over the air and a large crowd arrived on Saturday, July 13, 1946. Many remained overnight and others came on Sunday. The Show was of much interest, though it was not confined to daylilies. In the afternoon a meeting was held in the auditorium of the Seed House and the organization of the Midwest Hemerocallis Society was effected.

While the moving spirit was that of Mrs. Fischer, her sister, Jessie Shambaugh, Clarinda, Iowa, was chairman of the show and had a vital part in all that took place. It was she who wrote out the motion which was handed me to read: "We here today organize a Midwest Hemerocallis Society." The group that had formulated the plans which were presented consisted of Mrs. Shambaugh, Merritt Whitten, Marie

1-3. *The First National Robin*

STANDING, LEFT TO RIGHT: *Margaret Kane, Texas; Gretchen Harshbarger, Iowa; Ophelia Taylor, Florida; and Frances Rutledge, Missouri.*
Seated, left to right: Viola Richards, Indiana; Olive Hindman, Florida; Daisy Ferrick, Kansas.
Missing members from the picture: Fiffi Kline, Marie Anderson, and Gertrude Glynn.

Anderson, Daisy Ferrick, Olga Rolf Tiemann, Mary Claytor and Viola Richards.

The officers elected were: Mr. Whitten, president; Mrs. Shambaugh, vice president; Mrs. Ferrick, secretary; Frederick Fischer, treasurer; Mrs. Anderson, Round Robin secretary; Mrs. Richards, affiliation secretary; Mrs. Tiemann, publicity. The membership fee was set at $3.00 and Mrs. Claytor became the first charter member, Mrs. Fischer was number two and I was number three. I am now the oldest living charter member of the Society since Mrs. Claytor and Mrs. Fischer are deceased. Mrs. Ferrick says she was too busy taking in memberships to get an early number for herself.—VIOLA RICHARDS, 1956

In only six months following the meeting, Gretchen Harshbarger, daughter of Helen Field Fischer, edited the first *Yearbook* which gave more immediate reactions to the great event. Paul Frese, editor of *Flower Grower*, predicted an exciting future for the fledgling organization:

I do not know if you are aware as yet of just what you have discovered in your first Round Robin Convention held in Shenandoah. As I read the reports that have come to me, I believe that you have started an entirely new horticultural movement in the United States. . . .

Sometimes the sheer flow of adrenaline can overcome painful obstacles. Edna Hupp of Nebraska wrote to Mrs. Fischer on the day after:

Didn't someone say the flower people were crazy? Well, I really believe some of them are, especially me, for I'll tell you under what circumstances I came.

My husband owns and operates a Filling Station and Garage, so that evening I was up town finishing my plans and getting ice for flowers and making last minute arrangements, etc. The gas tank man was pumping gas in our tank underground. I had to stop a minute and discuss my going to the Flower Show with the young man, and a man walked up, lit a cigarette, and dropped the match in the fumes of gas covering an area of about 10 ft. square, (me in the middle). It exploded! It was only a few seconds duration, as thanks to the oil man he immediately grabbed the fire extinguisher and put out the blaze, but caught the right side of my dress on fire and burned my leg

1-4. *Gretchen Harshbarger, daughter of Frederick and Helen Field Fischer, editor of the* 1946 YEARBOOK, *and the second president of the Midwest Hemerocallis Society. She was a thoroughgoing professional, accomplished in many fields. (photo 1978)*

severely. I didn't sleep a wink Friday night, so got out as soon as daylight and picked my flowers and prepared to come to the Flower Show. The leg was awfully sore, and probably some noticed me limping, but I made it fine.

It was an inspiration to be one of such an enthusiastic crowd. I shall repeat what I so often say: 'There is no gift that is so precious as a beautiful memory.' For the continued memory of that day I am grateful!

Thanks to the power of radio, this meeting and flower show received advance publicity from coast to coast. The "party" turned out to be much bigger than anticipated. The activities were to catch the attention of the American Plant Life Society, whose members had a particular interest in *Hemerocallis*. It was from this group that AHS drew an impressive pool of scientific minds. More about this in later chapters "Registration" and "Discovery."

As for the Robins, they immediately established their position as holders of the most popular section in the new Society's *Journal* where their "excerpts" remain the undisputed favorite to this day.

As Charter Members Go

HE SOCIETY CHARTERED 556 members on its first outing. By the end of the year, membership had grown to 757. Steady growth, interspersed with occasional ups and downs, have brought the current membership tally to upwards of 9,500. Though the total membership has grown substantially, the charter member list is shrinking.

THE TENTH YEAR

On the occasion of the Society's tenth birthday, several charter members contributed remembrances to the 1956 *Yearbook*. Mrs. C. S. Hausen of Iowa recalls the 1946 meeting as being a happy occasion where flower fanciers became acquainted and "talked shop." The flower show was the most fondly reported event. Other charter members looked forward, backward, and sideways.

H. R. BURTNER (Maryland): For thirty years I have been interested in the hybridization of flowers. In 1939 I turned my full attention to hybridizing *Hemerocallis*. It was wonderful news, then years ago, when I heard the people of the Midwest were starting a daylily society.

1-5. *Stanley Saxton of Saratoga Springs, New York. Charter member and hybridizer of extra-hardy daylilies for the North.*

I think most of the folks who grew this fine garden and landscape flower realized the importance of a daylily society and the earlier members will remember the fine work of Mrs. Helen Field Fischer in getting it started.

LeMOINE J. BECHTOLD (Colorado): The American Hemerocallis Society has done an excellent job in bringing the work of all hybridizers before the public, interesting thousands of persons in growing daylilies in their gardens.

ROY V. ASHLEY (Michigan): One of my earliest childhood memories is of *Hemerocallis flava* growing with peonies and irises in my grandmother's garden in the early 1880s. . . .

About 1910 we began to receive catalogues from Bertrand Farr, then of Wyomissing, Pennsylvania. Some of these were real literary gems as well as listing much media for Farr iris, peonies, Oriental poppies, lilacs—and later, *Hemerocallis*. These were the first catalogues I had seen containing color plates. [It was the Farr Nursery that carried Arlow B. Stout's daylilies.]

MRS. DOUGLAS PATTISON: I am one of three charter members living in California. . . . I have greatly enjoyed the *Newsletters*, the highlights being the letters sent by Willard King, of Bethesda, Maryland. These were entertaining, interesting, and clearly descriptive.

MR. & MRS. HAROLD W. KNOWLTON (Massachusetts): Our interest in daylilies is an outgrowth of our iris garden and our visits to the garden of Mrs. Thomas Nesmith. In 1946 she told us of a proposed *Hemerocallis* society, and we applied for membership. That proposal fell through but the next year the Midwest Hemerocallis Society (now the American Hemerocallis Society) was formed and we joined as charter members. . . .

We are proud of our files of the nine *Yearbooks* of the Society. Particularly interesting are the articles on varieties from all parts of the country and the excerpts from letters of members and round robins.

MRS. ADOLPH RYBA (Illinois): We appreciate the *Yearbook* with its priceless information. It has been a joy to attend the national meetings where enduring friendships are made. A garden tour is an enjoyable occasion and frequently a profitable one, since one can make a firsthand appraisal of techniques and practices.

EUNICE FISHER (Wisconsin): Our tenth *Yearbook* issue constitutes a record of splendid progress. Surely there has been great improvement in *Hemerocallis* varieties. My enthusiasm for those I had in my garden in 1946 was very high, but my zest for the improved ones of today is even keener.

MRS. CLYDE SELL: Although Ohio was the home of one of America's earliest hem hybridists, Mr. C. Betscher, one can still drive hundreds of miles and see only 'Europa' growing along the highway or in clumps in neglected yards.

But the picture is changing. Within a ten-mile radius I note twenty gardens with a good showing of *Hemerocallis*.

GRETCHEN HARSHBARGER (Iowa): Never knew a more accomplished ten year old!

NOW WE ARE TWENTY

On the Society's twentieth birthday the charter member's were invited again to contribute commentary for publication, this time by sending in a brief letter about "What the daylily has meant to me." By this time charter members numbered 146. A total of 84 responses were received and published, making up 31 pages in the 1966 *Yearbook*. Friendships forged through a common interest placed first as the dominant theme of these letters. This was particularly true with the Round Robin members.

DAISY L. FERRICK (Kansas): One of the nicest things about this fascinating hobby is the lasting friendships formed through the years. Many of my dearest friends were met through the Round Robins because of our mutual love of the daylily.

MRS. PAUL KANE (Texas): . . . So, the daylily has come to mean friendship, a most precious gift, and especially so in the hurried days. I find relaxation comes easiest when spending a calm minute or so with a friend, discussing our mutual friend, the *daylily!*

MRS. FRED FLICK (Indiana): In considering what the daylily has meant to me I think first not of the ease of growing, nor the beauty of its blooms, nor its value in the landscape, nor the joy of breeding and growing its seedlings, but of friends.

Once members get caught up in hybridizing, however, more attention is directed back to the plant world. Comments are still effusive, and social benefits may be mentioned in passing, but there is evidence of a beginning obsession.

W. MILDRED BRADLEY (New York): The daylily has made me move and build a new house. My lakeside half-acre proved all too small, as I kept getting more daylilies, so a dozen years ago I built a new home among the trees I love in the hills. While there are 40 acres, the daylilies are spread out over three or four of them. There are probably thousands of plants, counting the seedlings, along with many of the older named varieties, of which there are well over 500.

O. R. HOWE, JR. (Massachusetts): Daylilies are my main interest in life. After a severe heart attack in 1945 I had to change my whole way of life and learn my limitations as well as have some absorbing interest. Simply raising flowers, which I had done all my life, was not enough. In 1941 I began raising daylilies and began a breeding program a year later and it was really stepped up in 1946 when I retired. . . .

Fortunately, I learned of the organization of the Midwest Hemerocallis Society and became a member, which was a help and encouragement to me.

PERCY I. MERRY (Massachusetts): Regardless of the results, there is a fascination and a thrill in hybridizing that nothing else brings. One of its by-products is the fact that it helps keep one young, since there is always something to anticipate. Last of all, the daylily has occupied two-thirds of my gardening time and thought.

Then there were those more caught up in peripheral interests.

M. FREDERICK STUNTZ (Massachusetts): Dr. Stout became one of my best friends during my work on the *Hemerocallis Check List*. I had been keeping a record of every new *Hemerocallis* as recorded in the *Yearbooks* of the American Amaryllis Society, now the American Plant Life Society, or in catalogs. When Mrs. Gretchen Harshbarger asked me to become the registrar of the Hemerocallis Society, I was happy to consent. My work with Dr. J.B.S. Norton on the *Descriptive Catalog of Hemerocallis Clones 1893 to 1948* was almost completed, so the task was simply to carry over the registrations in that volume until the publication of the complete *Hemerocallis Check List* in 1957.

While I enjoy working with the daylilies in my garden, nothing has ever given me greater satisfaction than doing that work [on the *Check Lists*].

L. Ernest Plouf (Boston, Massachusetts): I have a letter from Dr. Kraus at a time when he learned I had to go to war (WW2), in which he thanked me for having set him straight on some matters. He did not realize at that time, that the flowers must drop off promptly the day after bloom and that hardiness was very important, as well as keeping qualities.

For many years I have worked on a list of 100 Best Dormant Daylilies, divided between the seven blooming seasons here, the result of many breeders work, up to 1957.

Philip O. Buch (New Jersey): Hemerocallis need not always mean "Beautiful for a Day." To this end I have organized the Longevity Breeders' Robin which is doing something about it, thanks to my one-track mind and experience which I am happy to share. . . . [Mr. Buch introduced a line of "Tuday Lilies" bred for extended bloom into the second day.]

Pleasant associations were recorded by all 84 respondents. No . . . make that 83. Just as the soporific begins to take effect, a dissonant note is sounded.

Robert B. Wynne (North Carolina): Historically, I have observed with interest two decades of "growth and progress" in our hem patches. From a single-minded society, founded by the compassionate enthusiasm of Helen Field Fischer and others to a split complexity of flower-makers and rule-makers, from naive enjoyment of a simple effort—to misleading popularity polls, melon faddism, and competitive over-reach.

There have been moments of elation and days of euphoria. I've never been too tired to plant a new one or dig and ship an old one. I've reveled in the eyed, pinks, greens, the round, full forms, and candelabrum branching. Crossing and tagging. I've literally dropped in my own sweat; but twice in the past four years my seedlings have helped me learn to walk again and want to stay alive.

Now to turn the coin; I've sorrowed over fading reds and insubstantial tones of eggplant and puce. I've found but few daylilies without obvious shortcomings; I feel we need to concentrate more effectively on aesthetic selection in the seedling lines— and less on regional meetings, door prizes, auctions, top-heavy membership, or multiplying our chromosomes.

I must record honestly that all in all, daylilies have proved for me more trouble than triumph—expense, struggle, sacrifice. Unable by natural bent to maintain the cautionary attitude—to ooh and ahh and wheel and deal—I have been racked by collecting, crossing, hoping, hurting, testing, discarding. In short, I have endured the generative pangs of the determined hybridizer, an obsessive and arduous experience.

AT FIFTY — CHARTER MEMBERS TODAY

As the Society approaches its golden anniversary, only nine charter members remain on the records:

Howard S. Andros, New Hampshire; Arthur Blodgett, Wisconsin; Minnie Colquitt, Louisiana; Sarah Ellen Gillespie, Mississippi; Mrs. Gilbert Grapes, Nebraska; Mrs. Paul Kane, Texas; Emma Pederson, Nebraska; Stanley Saxton, New York; and Laura Sims, South Carolina.

Eight of the above responded to a brief questionnaire in the spring of 1994. Asked if they attended the 1946 meeting in Shenandoah, only Emma Pederson replied in the affirmative. (Charter membership remained open through the second annual meeting which was also held in Shenandoah.)

1. *What do you remember about the first meeting in Shenandoah?*

1-7. *Emma Pederson, charter member, taking notes at the Region One Meeting in 1992*

EMMA PEDERSON (Norfolk, Nebraska): The events included a flower show and everyone was to bring plants to share [give away]. I remember taking the white form of *Phlox divicata*. This was fairly new and Mr. Fischer [Helen Field Fischer's husband] admired the plant.

The Fischers cleared out a packing shed for the flower show. Some bloom scapes were shown, but mostly it was flower arrangements.

I appreciated so very much all that I had been taught by Helen Field Fischer on her radio program. She explained things so well. Yet she didn't want thanks for teaching—she said that you learned all that by yourself.

We took picnic lunches with us because in those days no restaurants were open on weekends. In fact, no businesses were open on weekends either. I believe we stayed in a rooming house that first year. Several hundred people attended.

The second meeting, also held in Shenandoah, was better than the first. I'm sure that more thought was put into it after the experiences of the first.

At one of the meetings, they held a game of identifying daylilies in one of the beds. Labels had been removed from the plants and those attending the meeting had to identify the plants. Esther Jessen and I kind of helped each other out—if I didn't know a variety, she did, and the other way around. We won the contest, but I don't remember what we got as a prize.

ARTHUR BLODGETT (Waukesha, Wisconsin): I didn't attend too many conventions as by visiting the numerous gardens close by I was well informed. Every year Ramona and I visited the Daylily Growers in the Chicago area starting with Dave Hall, Orville Fay, Brother Charles, and later, Jim Marsh, Nate Rudolph, Clarence Blocher, and Walter Jablonski.

MINNIE COLQUITT (temporarily in Denton, Texas): My *last* one was the Shreveport meeting. I enjoyed the extra lecture meeting on Hemerocallis—Garden Planting, and especially the slides of the Massachusetts (English) born lady. All my records and notes have been lost. [The "English-born" lady was Elsa Bakalar, a speaker at the Gardening Conference in 1992.]

2. How does the present Society compare to the early years?

HOWARD S. ANDROS (Walpole, New Hampshire): The growth of satellite daylily societies is welcomed today,

1-6. Minnie Colquitt, in a photo probably made in the late 1940s, about the time she became a charter member of the Society. A former registrar for the American Iris Society, she was interested in all kinds of plants. Before suffering a broken hip in 1994, she lived independently in the middle of her 40 acres in Louisiana. Of the photo, sent in by a friend, she says: "Marie Caillet told me of the picture. I NEVER saw THAT WOMAN in the picture. AGE is UNKIND!"

especially by the very young, the very old, and the very busy.

ARTHUR BLODGETT: The first I can remember is that by 4:00 P.M. the flowers were withered as they did not have enough substance to last out the day. Now some last till the next morning.

I just can't get over the rapid progress in the daylilies being introduced today, which have no comparison to those of several years past. I just wonder what the future holds.

MINNIE COLQUITT: So many "new" growers—too many introductions by amateur hybridizers; but the publications are much nicer. The recent registrations "floored" me—I personally knew Mr. Monroe and helped *start* the registration system.

SARAH E. GILLESPIE (Hattiesburg, Mississippi): Can't really say; rarely read AHS publications. I miss judging shows in Mobile and Mississippi Gulf Coast area, but things pass.

EMMA PEDERSON: Plants have been improved so much over the years. I purchased some of my first plants from Russell's in Texas, Zager in Des Moines, Iowa, and the Sass's in Omaha. I like the new daylilies that are round and full, with ruffles. Don't like the narrow petaled varieties, including the spiders. I'm still looking for a good pink.

STANLEY E. SAXTON (Saratoga Springs, New York): In general the activities of the Society are much the same now as at the start. The first *Yearbook* was almost as extensive as the present quarterly *Journals*. There was no charge at first for registration of daylily names. I started hybridizing several years before 1946 and had a sales catalog in 1945 with a roster of plants from Ralph Wheeler for whom I distributed introductions from 1945 to 1950. I even helped name his varieties. However, by the late 1940s I had a number of registered daylilies and had expanded my catalog greatly. [Mr. Saxton enclosed a copy of the 1955 catalog.] I attended most of the early conventions, joined robins and knew many of the members, especially those breeding new varieties, such as Dr. Stout, Mrs. Taylor and Mrs. Nesmith, Dr. Norton, etc. I have named about 300 daylilies to date (1994).

OTIS AND LAURA SIMS (Lexington, South Carolina): Mr. Sims and I are 98 and 99 years old now, but for many years we traveled all over the United States to the national meetings. We used that for an excuse to travel. It was wonderful meeting old friends and meeting new ones. The highlight of my life was when dear Hyta Mederer took two bus loads of flower lovers on a tour to Nova Scotia. We started at Walterboro, South Carolina headed for the state of Maine, stopping along the way to see daylily gardens. From Maine we boarded a big schooner, buses and all. Nova Scotia is one of the most beautiful places you would ever see.

3. *What would you like to see changed?*

HOWARD S. ANDROS: Nothing.

MINNIE COLQUITT: My physical ability to grow them! Would that I could. I once had *every* available *Hemerocallis* in England and Dr. Stout's from New York

Botanical Garden. Most of the species—Can you believe it!?!

STANLEY E. SAXTON: I think most of the changes that have been made were well thought out. I think it is difficult for breeders whose sales are predominantly regional and geared to conditions such as the breeders locale have difficulty getting votes for honors. My efforts have been in producing hardy dormant plants for the north. I would not expect to get votes from southern regions. Also, I grow few evergreens so would not vote for them which penalizes southern breeders.

4. *Are you still growing daylilies?*

HOWARD S. ANDROS: You bet.

ARTHUR BLODGETT: I am still growing a small up-to-date collection and am more dedicated to breeding than any time in the past as I can no longer travel.

The garden work keeps me busy. I am lucky to have my grandson Mike Blodgett do most of the work.

Just this year I had a seedling bloom on a single plant which is the finest bloom I have ever seen and am still looking to the future.

Daylilies and the Society are surely growing.

MINNIE COLQUITT: Recently sold my garden [in Louisiana] and it breaks my heart.

Sorry this is late. Illness has moved me from one place to another—*but* I'm doing well and expect to "read" gardening, though I'll have no plans to grow them.

SARAH E. GILLESPIE: Yes, but not collecting anymore. All my varieties are old, but still beautiful in the garden.

EMMA PEDERSON: Yes, I'm still very much growing daylilies and have a good modern collection. I am 89 years old and still do all my own gardening. I attend most of our Nebraska Daylily Society meetings and don't miss many Region One meetings.

STANLEY E. SAXTON: I grow approximately 1600 daylilies and sell widely both of my own and others.

OTIS AND LAURA SIMS: Yes. I have nine hundred named varieties and a good many of the newest ones, but I am not able to do much, so I am about at the stopping place. Mr. Sims is in the V.A. Hospital in not too good shape, I'm sorry to say. [Ed. note: Otis Sims died in October 1994.]

Thank you for remembering the charter members.

Chapter 2

An Organization Grew

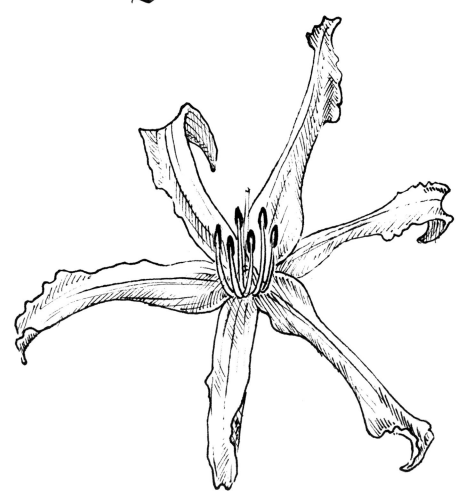

A shared interest is a wonderful catalyst.
Rich and poor, old and young, the wise and foolish meet on
common ground and find pleasure in the association.
OPHELIA TAYLOR

Getting Down To Business

PAUL FRESE, PAST EDITOR of the now defunct *Flower Grower* magazine, wrote to commend the new Midwest Hemerocallis Society for its "Robin Convention" held in Shenandoah in 1946. He ended his letter with an interesting statement:

> *Too many of our current conventions are too much concerned with business matters.*

Any draftee who has weathered an epic board meeting will likely concur. Yet history has shown that groups soon disperse without organization. It follows that business matters are a necessary part of organization, like them or not. Ideally, they provide an invisible framework to distribute the load.

THE NAME OF THE GAME

During the first eight years of its existence, the Society underwent three name changes. The founding organizational name, Midwest Hemerocallis Society, reflected the modest aspirations of the 1946 Round Robin party in Shenandoah.

Soon it became apparent that interest extended far beyond the confines of the Midwest, and in 1948 the membership voted to change the name to The Hemerocallis Society. This event was marked by the adoption of the Society's first simple constitution, drawn up by Pearl Sherwood and committee.

In 1954, the organization took its present name, American Hemerocallis Society, Inc. This action was taken for economic reasons. In order to effect a savings in postage, the Society was to be incorporated in Le Mars, Iowa, in 1955. (When the Society received its nonprofit status in 1979, another substantial savings was realized.)

Will this be the final change? Only "The Shadow" knows. Almost from the beginning the AHS has had an active foreign membership. Some have suggested "International Hemerocallis Society" as a more appropriate title. The latest rumblings indicate a preference for "American Daylily Society." This writer prefers the present inclusion of "Hemerocallis" in the name—not for botanically snobbish reasons, but because it generates so much curiosity! How many times have other guests at a convention hotel stopped to ask about the *disease* we represent on our name tags. It is a perfect opening to explain that while it may become a disease, it starts as a beautiful flower.

A VIEW FROM THE TOP

As surely as a party happens, dirty dishes follow. Someone must be drafted to act as K.P.

The bulk of the work in the first five years fell on the officers, who at that time accounted for the Society's total administration. The president had the task of appointing the various officers and committee heads. All too often, suitable persons could not be found quickly enough to fill crucial vacancies, whereupon the president evolved into something of a factotum. With no board of directors, this amounted to a crushing responsibility.

GETTING GOOD HELP

The presidential experience was made more tolerable with the aid of devoted helpers. D.R. McKeithan of Oklahoma was surely one of these. More than one president acknowledged his orderly mind by assigning to him highly critical, detailed tasks. His hand helped shape the Constitution & Bylaws, the Awards & Honors program, and the budget committee. Documents were scrutinized, tested, and revised from 1950 until 1960. Thus evolved a basically sound organizational structure that was little changed for many years. Indeed, some "improvements" have underscored the wisdom of the original plan.

Had Dave McKeithan been performing as a soloist, the work might have proceeded more quickly. However, there was an orchestra, and it was not always in tune. Regarding the Awards and Honors program, Dave describes a certain disaccord:

Geddes Douglas, Bob Allen, Bob Schreiner and Mrs. Nesmith wanted it to be an exact copy of the system used by the American Iris Society. Wilmer Flory, Viola Richards, Maria Marcue, Howard Hill and others wanted something different. I got caught in the middle of this squabble because in late 1950 President Bess Ross asked me to intervene and come up with a sound and effective recommendation. It was some time before all the parties involved reached a middle-ground compromise and the program was adopted.

The work on the revised constitution was begun in 1952 at the behest of then-president Edgar Rice of Oklahoma. When Mrs. Marcue took office in 1954 the Society was being incorporated. During that period, the versatile Dave McKeithan was serving as First Vice President and Chairman of the Awards and Honors Committee. He remembers it as a trying, though productive, era:

> Thinking that I did not have enough to do, Mrs. Marcue made me her advisor. Truly, these were the formative years and many loose ends had to be tied together to make our Society an effective, mature organization. At this time, it should be noted that our membership was below the 2,000 goal and funds were limited. There was no compensation to anyone except a very small stipend for the editor and secretary. Sometimes I wonder how we survived as there were no travel expenses for officers and directors.

Officers and Directors

HERE ARE STILL NO TRAVEL EXPENSES for officers and directors. That is, none that emanate from the national level. More recently, some regions have begun to provide subsidy to assist their directors with travel costs. Directors are required to attend two meetings each year, one of which is held at the AHS National Convention.

Another facet of the board that has not changed is its function as a working board. The comments of President Richard Peck in 1966 still apply:

> Most boards of directors that I know are not working boards; they are policy-making boards, whose work is usually limited to ratifying the results of the work of others.
>
> Not so the AHS Board. Aside from two special committees chaired and manned by members-at-large, each board member chairs one or more standing or special committees and the work devolves upon the board member who reports at each of the two annual meetings.

Because the first rudimentary constitution had no provision for a body of directors, much serious study was given to the 1950 revision of the Constitution & Bylaws. By decree of the new document, inaugural terms were adjusted to coincide with the calendar year. Norman Goss retired under the old constitution, following the annual summer meeting, and Bess Ross moved up from vice-president to serve a brief but intense term as president in the latter part of 1950. Thus the actual formation of the first AHS Board of Directors fell upon her shoulders.

Mrs. Ross's task in assembling the first board of directors shared some elements common to the biblical Cain's search for a wife. Both required a certain amount of creativity in working from scratch. The new constitution called for 12 directors. Nominees chosen from four broad segments of the United States were presented to the membership via one of the Society's quarterly publications. In due course, mail ballots were sent out, returned, and counted. Those who were elected were called together in St. Louis for the first board of directors meeting. Eight members attended and the serious organizational work began.*

---

*The complete slate of the first board of directors were 12 in number: Robert E. Allen, Elmer A. Claar, Philip G. Corliss, Geddes Douglas, Olive Hindman, J.W. House, George E. Lenington, Edwin C. Munson, J.B.S. Norton, F. Edgar Rice, Bess Ross, and Robert E. Schreiner.

photo by Harvey Horne

> The Board of Directors
> In noticed seclusion,
> Debated and voted
> In utter confusion.
> . . . .
> GEDDES DOUGLAS, 1952
> *(member of the first board)*

2-1. The 1995 board of directors prepare for a day of "noticed seclusion." Staff and off-board committee chairmen are included in this photo. Back row standing: Bill White (General Counsel), Ken Cobb, Elly Launius (Executive Secretary), Earlene Garber, Dwaine Kurtz, Bill Reinke (Non-Current Publications), Harvey Horne (Slides & Video), Mary Houston (Exhibition & Judges' Clinics), Jim Brennan, Dan Trimmer (Display Gardens). Center row, across table: Jack Harrison, Larry Harder, Fran Neale, Hal Rice, Frances Gatlin (Editor), Curtis High. Front row seated: George Forsythe, Earnest Yearwood, Bob McConnell, Mary Gage, Bertie Ferris (Protocol), Bob Wing, Harry Harwood.

The board selection process provided by the 1950 Bylaws was rather interesting. It required an election by mail ballot. A presidential committee of three, appointed yearly, drew up a slate, taking into consideration regional representation. The list of nominees was sent to all members. Within a specified period after receipt of the list, any twenty members (so long as no more than ten were from one region) could make nominations as they wished and forward them to the AHS Secretary for inclusion on the ballot. The ballot was then mailed to the entire membership.

The difficulties of implementation and expenses incurred gradually eroded that first idealistic plan. By 1955 the mail ballot had disappeared and the vote was taken at the annual business meeting. By 1988, the AHS Board of Directors had long since become a self-perpetuating body. It was made up of 15 members, in effect chosen *by the governing board*, to loosely represent the 15 AHS regions of the continental United States. Terms were for three years, as they are today, and could be optionally extended

by a second term. In 1988 the board—with a little nudge from the membership—chose the more democratic path of placing the selection of directors in the hands of the regions which they represent. The new system has generated more interest, even competition, in national affairs and likely accounts for the recent trend toward regional subsidy of travel expenses for members of the board.

THE NATIONAL OFFICERS

The important 1950 revision of the Constitution and Bylaws provided for specific officers elected from and by its own number: (1) a President, (2) First Vice-President, (3) Second Vice-President, (4) Third Vice-President, (5) Secretary, and (6) Treasurer. Each vice-presidency was tied to a specific board chairmanship. With the exception of the office of secretary, this slate of officers remained constant until 1993 at which time the Society retained only one national Vice-President whose position was not tied to a specific chairmanship. Until recently, AHS

photo courtesy Carol Skinner

2-2.
*Daisy Ferrick,
first secretary/
treasurer of the
original Midwest
Hemerocallis
Society. She
served a later
term as secretary
when the name
was changed to
the American
Hemerocallis
Society.*

AHS PRESIDENTS

Merritt Whitten	1946–1947
Gretchen Harshbarger	1948
George Lenington	1949
Norman P. Goss	Jan.–Aug., 1950
Bess Ross	Aug.–Dec., 1950
Joseph House	1951
F. Edgar Rice	1952–1953
Maria Marcue	1954–1956
Wilmer B. Flory	1957–1958
Hubert A. Fischer	1959–1961
Annie T. Giles	1962–1963
George P. Watts	1964
Richard C. Peck	1965–1966
George T. Pettus	1967–1968
Bertie Ferris	1969
Pearl Hancock	1970–1971
Luther J. Cooper, Jr.	1972–1973
Betty Barnes	1974–1975
R.W. Munson, Jr.	1976
Martha Hadley	1977
Clarence J. Crochet	1978–1979
Luke Senior, Jr.	1980–1981
Ned Irish	1982–1983
Bill Ater	1984–1985
Selma Timmons	1986–1987
Annie Weinreich	1988–1989
Dorothea Boldt	1990–1991
Nell Jessup	1992–1993
Ken Cobb	1994–1995
Earlene Garber	1996

Presidents have borne the responsibility of recommending their own successors. A 1995 Bylaws revision provides for a board-elected nominating committee to make the recommendation. A simple majority vote by the board constitutes election.

THE SECRETARY

Daisy Ferrick of Topeka, Kansas, was a charter member, present at the organizational meeting in Shenandoah, where her skills were immediately put to use taking memberships. She was elected secretary of the newly formed Midwest Hemerocallis Society and served a one-year term. She was re-elected as secretary of the incorporated American Hemerocallis Society in 1954. At the end of 1959 she retired, saying that she could not continue working for the salary the new Society was able to pay. She remained an interested and active member, however, throughout her long life. Up to the time of Daisy's retirement, the secretary's position was that of an officer; but when her replacement, Olive Hindman, was installed in 1960, it was as a staff member.

A nominal change to the office of secretary was made in 1987 when the board conferred on it the title of AHS Executive Secretary. The change merely reflected the scope of the work already being performed. Duties have increased in parallel to the volume of membership.

The Society has enjoyed two other lengthy periods of secretarial stability: from 1978-1985 served by Joan Senior, and from 1987 forward, filled by the current executive secretary, Elly Launius.

2-3.
*Elly Launius,
Jackson,
Mississippi.
One of the
Society's
long-term
secretaries,
she has
served since
1987.*
(Photo 1995)

photo by Frances Gatlin

2-4. *Post-presidential activities. Betty Barnes, Bertie Ferris, Clarence Crochet enjoying life at Orlando Convention in 1994.*

photo courtesy Seniors

2-5. *Former President Luke Senior with former long-term AHS Secretary Joan Senior, photographed in 1994. During Luke's extended term on the board, he served as both treasurer and president. Throughout much of the same period, Joan Senior was employed as secretary. While this particular arrangement served the Society well, the board later adopted a policy disallowing two AHS employees or employee/board members in the same household. (The word "household" is descriptive of the Society's office arrangements, past and present. Officers and employees provide their own office space, usually carved out of a niche in the home.)*

Joan Senior was the last AHS secretary to struggle with an addressograph machine. The "pre-owned" model may have been an improvement over the typewriter, but its metal plates and chains and pulleys were in need of constant attendance. It was Luke who found himself in yet another position of service to AHS—under the table adjusting the pulleys. Because of the noise associated with plate making, heavy tray-loads of plates were carted to the porch for cutting. "It sounded just like a concrete mixer," Luke laughed.

The year following Joan's retirement in 1985, the board authorized purchase of a computer for the office of secretary.

The Regions

EGIONS WERE A NATURAL evolution of a Society that was destined in short order to overflow the boundaries of its own continent. While little has been done to define geographically the international membership—beyond assigning it the designation of Region 20—domestic divisions have moved from an official ten to fifteen (figure 2-6).

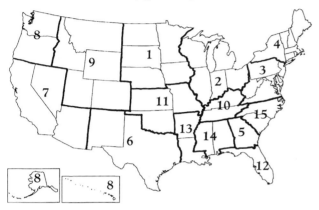

2-6. Present-day regional divisions in the United States (1995). Alaska and Hawaii (inset) are a part of Region 8. For administrative and bookkeeping purposes, foreign countries are designated as Region 20.

One of the first acts of the Society in 1948, upon dropping the inadequate provincial "Midwest" of its title, was to establish 10 regions. The divisions were based on area, population, and climate. (See map, figure 2-7 below.)

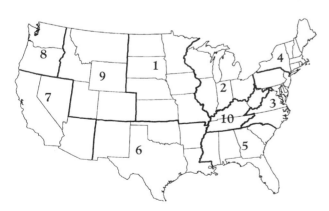

2-7. The ten regions established in 1948 when the organization's name changed to The Hemerocallis Society.

To each region, a Regional Director was appointed. At least that was the long-range plan. One year later only nine had been placed and then it was time for a new plan. Major changes were in store when the Bylaws were revised to cover the Society's incorporation as the American Hemerocallis Society. At that time the regional boundaries were redrawn to make 12 regions (figure 2-8).

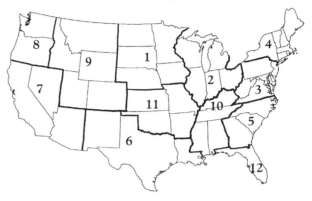

2-8. Realignment of regions under the 1950 bylaws which adopted the name American Hemerocallis Society, Inc. Canadian members were asked to affiliate with the regions adjoining them. (1951)

At the same time, "Regional Directors" became "Regional Supervisors" and were joined by Publicity Directors. The new title Regional Supervisor came vested with a great deal of responsibility. It was the intent of the board to establish a strong link to the membership through this office that would become today's Regional Vice-President. The Regional Supervisors would comprise a Board of Counselors whose duty was "to advise and counsel the Board of Directors on all matters relating to the best interests of the Society and to convey to members of the Society all information and advice relating to the administration of the Society." (1950 AHS Bylaws; author's italics.) The national First Vice-President of the Society acted as presiding officer of the Board of Counselors.

In 1959, the region heads were again renamed when they became Regional Vice-President (RVP) and Regional Publicity Director (RPD), titles that have endured to the present.

Regions themselves stabilized also, in the geographic sense. By 1959 there were 15 regions. Only two realignments, both in the southern states, have occurred since. Foreign membership was later designated as Region 20.

INTERNATIONAL MEMBERS

Even as a very young Society, AHS enjoyed association with members from countries outside the United States. After all, the species were rooted in Asian countries and hybridizing of daylilies began in England. Some of our early hybridizers, including Arlow Burdette Stout, were in close touch with botanists and plant breeders of other countries during the early part of the century. The more mature American Iris Society led the way with contacts as some of its members embraced the daylily. Even World War II had the side effect of establishing harmonious communication between nations. "Networking" has a long tradition in plant societies.

When Hubert Fischer was president of the Society from 1959 through 1961, he had considerable foreign correspondence that led quite naturally to his being placed at the new post of Foreign Secretary for AHS. What followed was an amazing 20 years of détente that spanned the globe. In 1976 Mr. Fischer recorded his reminiscences for the *Journal*. This man was everywhere!

...(There is) a great deal of interest in England due to the late Harry Randall who grew many American

2-9. Hubert Fischer, first Foreign Secretary, also served as AHS President.

2-10. Lady Cynthia Carew-Pole of Cornwall. As a member of AHS, she attended conventions and lectured in the United States in the 1960s. During her lifetime she had one of the largest Hemerocallis collections in England. The National Trust now holds a residual collection of 550 cultivars, planted all around the grounds at Antony House. A "Daylily Day" is planned for peak bloom.

daylilies in his garden in Beconsfield and Lady Cynthia Carew-Pole who has the Antony House Nursery at Torpoint, Cornwall. . . . In Germany there is a great deal of activity. We first sent plants to Hamburg in 1960 for the exhibition at Internationale Gartenbau Austellung which were judged in 1963. When I visited there that spring the plants showed good care and were growing well. . . . Herman Hald, President of the German Iris and Lily Society has been most helpful. . . . Graffen Helen Von Stein Zeppelin who has visited in our country several times has probably the most comprehensive collection in her nursery in Laufen, Germany. [Several other German contacts are mentioned.] . . . The most important contact that I have had in France has been with Jean Cayeaux, grandson of the famous iris breeder of years ago. . . . I had been in contact with Austria since 1956 when I sent seeds over. . . . I tried to get to the Italian Iris Society there to also start trials for daylilies in addition to their International Iris Competition, and while interested, lack of funds made this impossible. . . . My first contact with Holland was in 1959 when we had an invitation for the society to participate in the 1960 Floriade. While the time was short, we decided to do so. . . . (When) he suggested that I come to the International Botanical Congress which would be held in Leningrad in July of 1975 I decided to go. . . . I was presented with three paintings of the daylilies and later invited to dinner at the home of Dr. [Tatyana] Turchinskaya. She had written a book on *Hemerocallis* which was published in 1973 containing ninety pages with some color plates of species. . . . I had been sending seeds to Australia since 1968. . . . I had been corresponding since 1964 and had sent packets of seeds including tetraploid. At that time he [Sam Rix] wrote: "At present daylilies are a rare sight in New Zealand gardens." [and later] He had distributed plants and seeds throughout New Zealand. . . . I first met Dr. Shuicho Hirao in Europe and for many years we exchanged letters, seeds and plants, he sending Japanese Iris and Hosta plants and seeds and I to him iris and daylily plants and seeds. . . . Dr. Hirao had made arrangements for a repeat program in Tokyo where the huge audience was a bit frightening. The daylilies seem to attract special attention. One elderly gentleman said to me later, to think that they have been growing on our doorstep for all these years. . . . In some countries it has been very frustrating. One request for seeds from Latvia in 1972 had been filled with a letter and seeds sent air mail. Later a tearful reply that the seeds had been removed by the powers that be and the form sent to me that he was notified "seeds taken out for destruction and burned in the stove." . . . There has been no problem getting seeds through to Czechoslovakia . . . nor has there been any problem with Lithuania. . . . In early 1964 I received a letter from Friedersdorf in East Germany addressed to me only to Chicago but it managed to reach me [and we complain about the post office!]. . . . Switzerland has been very active in their society, Iris and Lily Friends. . . . Other countries from which I have received correspondence are Denmark, Africa, Rhodesia, and from our neighbors to the south, Mexico, Brazil, Argentina, Honduras, Costa Rica, Columbia and recently a new member in Venezuela. I have lost contact with India, Poland, Israel, and Spain. . . . I am in need of a fairly large amount of seeds for a project in Japan and would be grateful for your help.

So goes a day in the life of an AHS Foreign Secretary, or International Secretary as the position is now known.

In 1982, the Society was fortunate to secure the services of Bob Bearce (Park Ridge, Illinois) as Mr. Fischer's replacement. The new secretary also had international connections through his work and maintained a heavy correspondence as well as personal contacts through international visits. Correspondence was an ingrained habit with Bob, who was already a prodigious letter writer and former Round Robin Chairman. As an established hybridizer, Bob also harvested many seeds from his own choice crossings to distribute worldwide.

In 1991 Roswitha Waterman of New York assumed the position of International Secretary. It was a natural extension of her already active role as daylily ambassador to Germany. For several years she made annual pilgrimages to her native country where she generated much interest through her slide shows held in Germany and Belgium. In 1993, she was awarded the first AHS Regional Service Award for service performed in Region 20.

Today, independent daylily societies such as Hemerocallis Europa and the Hemerocallis Society of Australia reflect the popularity of the daylily abroad. Australia has begun its own journal. Canadian membership has tripled in a short time and those members have applied to AHS for status as a separate region within AHS. If growth continues, a broader framework will have to be laid to accommodate it. Meanwhile, the Horticultural Society of Pakistan has displayed a keen interest in growing and hybridizing daylilies.

The AHS collects seeds which are donated by hybridizers and distributed by the AHS International Secretary for the purpose of assisting members in other countries who need help in getting started with daylilies. With almost 300 foreign members in 26 countries, the International Secretary is kept busy posting seeds, letters and, perhaps most important, good will.

2-11. *Francois Verhardt, currently active AHS member in Belgium, awarded the AHS Regional Service Award for his continuing efforts to popularize daylilies throughout Europe.*

2-12. *From left: Gretchen Harshbarger, second president of the Midwest Hemerocallis Society and editor of the first Yearbook; her mother, Helen Field Fischer, who sounded the call that brought daylily lovers together at Shenandoah in July, 1946; Hans P. Sass, Nebraska hybridizer and winner of the first Stout Medal; Merritt Whitten, first president of the Society, and editor of the 1948 Yearbook. (Test Garden at Shenandoah.)*

EARLY EXPERIMENTS WITH TEST GARDENS

For the first few years, Helen Field Fischer acted as reporter for the test garden in Shenandoah. Then in 1952 she wrote:

> We no longer call the garden at Shenandoah a "Test Garden" for we have no resident member qualified to give accurate, technical judging such as that which gives such satisfaction and pleasure to those who sent plants to Valleevue. It is merely a show garden, but it has excellent cultivation, and name stakes, and is in a spot easily accessible and is seldom without visitors. We now have 350 varieties.
>
> Last summer we were submerged by a flood, during which two of our beds containing new and very valuable varieties were under water for fully a week; but they bloomed well at the usual time and this spring we find that every plant in these beds is alive and unusually husky looking. All of the plants have made good growth. . . .
>
> We have never forgotten the wise and lengthy letter that Mr. Wheeler wrote to us when we asked for plants—and advice. He warned us of the difficulty of finding skilled help; of keeping name stakes in place; and of controlling the growth of extra robust varieties. He will be glad to know that our Ben Darby has personally made and painted every stake; removed any wayward varieties; keeps a careful card index as well as a plat book, and that in the blooming season he can name promptly any flower that you present from the show garden. Your best way of showing your appreciation is to plan to send him promptly plants of your new introductions which will add to the glory of this show garden where he teaches people to appreciate this beloved flower.
>
> —HELEN FIELD FISCHER

AHS sponsored other test gardens in the early years. Those in Ohio (Valleevue), Oklahoma, and Louisiana are on record. But the difficulties that Ralph Wheeler cited, coupled with a burgeoning list of introductions, spelled doom for official test gardens under the aegis of a young society with such limited resources. To date they have not been reinstated, although many official Display Gardens are open to public viewing.

Conventions

HE FIRST "CONVENTION"—the Round Robin gathering that resulted in the formation of the Midwest Hemerocallis Society—was attended by a large number of people. The exact record has been difficult to pin down, but a conservative estimate appears to be well over a thousand.

It should be understood that a relatively small percentage of visitors came with the intent of forming a daylily society. Although instigated by the daylily Round Robins, "Operation Hem Show" did not exclude other plant material. The "thousands" of visitors that arrived were lured by the promise of a flower show which invited display of beautiful and varied arrangements. Robin leader Marie Anderson and her troops acted as show guides. Those interested in forming a Society stayed for what might be considered the first annual daylily business meeting.

The next two annual meetings of the newly organized Hemerocallis Society were also held in Shenandoah. An ecumenical flavor pervaded these events as the second meeting shared space with the Penstemon Society. Both organizations were permitted to "broadcast" from the Field Radio Station KFNF. Then at the invitation of Edgar Rice and Dave McKeithan, the meeting shifted to Bartlesville, Oklahoma, and it has been rotated, by invitation, among other locations since that time.

While the annual business meeting is required by constitution, garden tours are required by members. It is the opportunity to tour exceptional gardens that brings members together. There they can observe and evaluate firsthand the newer daylilies. Most tour gardens contain fine collections of new as well as classic daylilies. These are often supplemented by guest plants from hybridizers.

Another strong attraction of conventions is the social aspect. To some, it is the primary reason for attending. Rain may dampen the bloom, and the order of business may hold little interest; but new and renewed friendships are always for the taking at national conventions.

Attendance has had its ups and downs. During the first years, every convention had an enthusiastic

photo by Frances Gatlin

2-13. People and daylilies—an irresistible mix. The Turnock garden, Pittsburgh convention, 1993.

turnout. Then in 1962, *Journal* editor Wilmer Flory noted a decline:

The percentage of our members attending the national conventions has fallen off in recent years. From comments heard at recent conventions and elsewhere, it would seem that there are several contributing factors. Steadily mounting costs—both financial and in terms of time lost—seem to account for most of the fall-off in attendance figures. The growing popularity of the shorter, less expensive Regional Conventions may have had its effect also. Then, too, there are those who used to attend the National Conventions but now take the same amount of money and take leisurely daylily treks from South to North during the blooming season, and have a grand time doing it. And finally, there is a growing reluctance on the part of breeders and introducers to send their finest new things to the National Tour Gardens. . .

The causes and effect cited by Wilmer Flory are extant today. The only difference lies in growth of membership. Now, a relatively small percentage of attending membership can result in a crowd of 700-800. The mechanics of handling these larger numbers places strictures on the host club and visitors alike. It is now possible for friends to attend the same meeting and never find one another!

Outstanding regional meetings, both in season and out, may be satisfying the needs of members for fellowship and economy. However, so long as major issues are voted and approved at the annual business meeting, it is essential that the National Conventions have a representative turnout. What better occasion to combine business with pleasure?

NO ROOM AT THE INN

Just how much has the cost of conventions increased? At the first Shenandoah gathering, Round Robineers stayed over free of charge as guests of the Henry Field Seed & Nursery Company. Cots were set up in a large area of the main nursery building to serve as a temporary dormitory. For the third annual convention held in Shenandoah in 1948, members were asked to secure rooms at one of the two hotels in town. A Society publication lists the price of accommodations:

The Delmonico Hotel
Single room (1 person), $2.00, with water but without toilet
Single room (1 person), $3.00 to $3.75 (with bath and toilet)
Twin beds in plain room with water only, $3.00
Twin beds with bath and toilet, $5.00

Waubansie Hotel
Without bath - 1 person $1 .75; 2 persons, $3.50
With bath $2.50; 2 persons, $3.50

Thanks to a series of colossal jubilees sponsored by the two seed companies, Shenandoah was accustomed to overflow crowds. Homeowners took such occasions as an opportunity to pocket a little extra change. Children were given pallets on the floor while their beds were temporarily let to visitors. The kids loved it and everybody went away happy.

Fifty years later, there are *three* motels in Shenandoah.

Chapter 3
Winning Ways

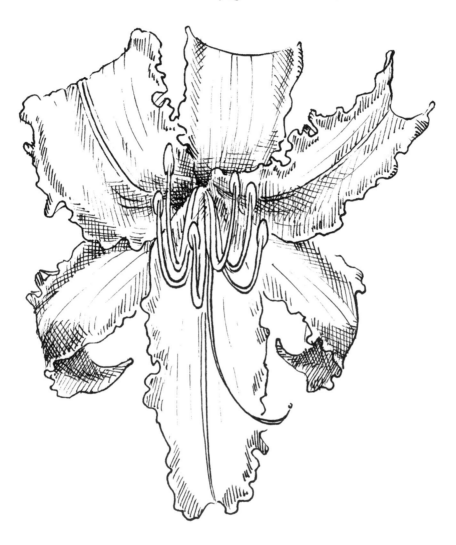

Anybody can win,
unless there happens to be a second entry.
GEORGE ADE

The Show Must Go On

XHIBITIONS OR ACCREDITED SHOWS have played a dominant role in the AHS since the occasion of the 1946 gathering in Shenandoah, Iowa. The Shenandoah exhibit was not the first daylily show, however. That milestone occurred six years earlier and was reported in *Herbertia* by Wyndham Hayward, one of the three organizers of the American Amaryllis Society: "The first competitive all-daylily show in the history of the world was conducted by the American Amaryllis Society April 18–19, 1940 at the Mead Botanical Garden in Orlando-Winter Park, Florida." Another feather in that much-decorated cap.

The 1946 show, a cornerstone in the AHS's history, was planned and executed by members of the First Round Robin in cooperation with the Henry Field Seed Company. It was a primary drawing card for the historic event that spawned the Midwest Hemerocallis Society. Recalling the excitement generated by that first show, the 1946 *Yearbook* describes it as

> a show without premiums, without judges, and without expense. The exhibits were brought by the visitors, and visiting experts answered questions and wrote labels.

Attendants could exhibit any arrangements they chose. Exhibits ran the gamut from rock garden plants to a collection of choice rex begonias. The eclectic nature of the show fostered lasting friendships based on a common appreciation of beauty.

The daylily table was in the charge of First Round Robin leader Marie Anderson and Ben Darby, an industrious young man who provided the muscle for the Shenandoah Daylily Test Garden. Operation Hem Show brought in an overflow house. Postwar gardeners were ready for a big flower show.

Juanita Jorgensen, member of the above Robin, describes the morning of the first day when "the public advanced by the hundreds and poured through every breach." Many visitors who had a slight prejudice against "Corn Lilies" went away chastened, she reports with thinly disguised glee.

In the years to follow, the new American Hemerocallis Society laid the groundwork for more structured exhibitions. The Nickerson Color Fan was adopted as a guide for setting up show classifications. In 1951 Mrs. A.S. Hansen became the first AHS Exhibition Chairman. She was succeeded the following year by Philip G. Corliss, author of a popular book of the day, *Hemerocallis, The Perennial Supreme.* Dr. Corliss served as chairman for two years during which time he introduced show rules and point scoring.

Mrs. Guy Rice, chairman from 1955 to 1956, compiled the first *Judges' Handbook.* Clinics were stressed. Over the years, subsequent changes to show rules have necessitated several additions and revisions to the first handbook. Inventive minds and action-oriented leadership almost guarantee a law of perpetual motion where handbooks are concerned. Following are publications to date:

1955	First Judges' Handbook	Mrs. Guy Rice
1959	Supplement	Frances Lamb
1964	Revision	Bertie Ferris
1975	Revision	Bertie Ferris
1982	Revision	B.F. Ater
1987	Revision	Dorothea Boldt
1990	Revision	Ken Cobb

A major overhaul of show regulations and exhibition clinics took place in the early 1990s under the leadership of Nell Jessup and Ken Cobb. Clinics were expanded from one to three levels and a new loose-leaf manual detailed many changes. While there was a general tightening up of requirements for judges, some welcome changes were introduced in the shows themselves. At long last the alphabetized show was given legitimacy. This was a relief to classification committees who had struggled for years with "baby-ribbon pink" syndrome and other elusive interpretations. Still, some local societies preferred the old color-class system and, happily for all, AHS found it could coexist with diversity.

Accredited shows are given latitude to tailor their schedules to existing circumstance. For example, special sections may be added if they do not conflict with AHS standards. However, to be accredited, shows *must* include certain sections. When the groundwork rules were laid in the late 1950s, five sections were required in the show schedule. Now there are nine. AHS Rosettes are awarded to winners in Sections 1–8. Section 9 is a competition for the Achievement Medal.

In 1957 the rotating Mabel Yaste Tricolor Trophy was established to encourage interest in the artistic division of shows. Rules governing this award were not finalized until 1960. The trophy continued to rotate until all spaces for engraving winners' names were used. In 1980 the silver bowl was retired and replaced with a non-rotating medal, now called the AHS Tricolor Medal.

In the early days, *American Home Magazine* offered an Achievement Medal which carried the name of the donor until the magazine discontinued its funding in 1960. This had been a popular, prestigious award, for it signified the pinnacle of a show division that permitted hybridizers to test their wares. Then in 1961, major funding by the Chicago Convention Committee and an anonymous donor assured the medal's continuance for several years. The AHS Achievement Medals are now paid for by the Society.

The Ophelia Taylor Horticultural Medal was made available for accredited shows by Region 12 in 1966. The purpose of this award was to stress horticultural procedures. Loosely stated, the award is contingent upon accumulated point scores.

The Gold and Silver Bole Medals are not AHS awards but they are available to qualifying show

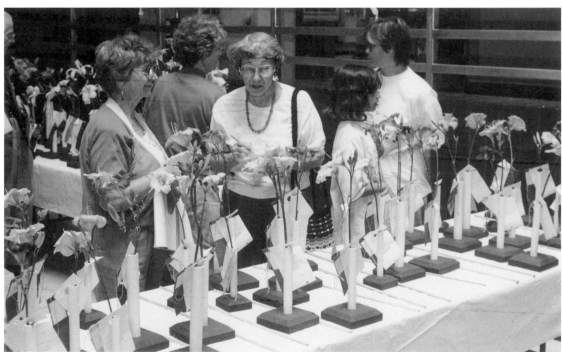

photo by Harvey Horne

3-1. *A flower show in progress. Similar shows throughout the United States and other countries are open to the public. They allow thousands of visitors a close-up view of the advances in the development of the daylily. Most shows feature an educational table with display material and free handouts. (Raleigh, North Carolina.)*

participants of various horticultural societies, including the AHS. They are sponsored by the American Horticultural Society for the purpose of encouraging horticultural excellence.

JUDGES

Accredited shows require a battery of judges schooled in the ways of horticultural excellence. Judges' Clinics predate Garden Judges' Workshops by several years and are dedicated to different principles. The two groups have often been confused—so much so that the original designation of Awards & Honors Judge was changed to Garden Judge, in the vain hope of defining the territory. Garden judging is done in the garden and Exhibition judging is done at accredited shows. Accreditation as an Exhibition Judge carries some rather exacting responsibilities.

THE BOTTOM LINE

Daylily flower shows are popular with AHS members as well as outsiders. In a recent report, the total accredited shows alone reached 54 for a single season. More than 53,000 visitors poured into these shows. The figures do not take into account a large number of unjudged exhibitions.

Anyone who has been directly involved in staging one of these shows knows that they do not run on autopilot. Surely every harried show chairman or the chief bottle washer must at some low moment have wavered before the opening curtain.

It all comes together on show day. Even the most disgruntled worker has to admire the display. Perhaps after 50 years there are fewer visitors who think in terms of "Corn Lilies," but shows still draw many neophyte viewers. Flower shows probably offer the single most effective vehicle for spreading the gospel of daylilies.

Awards & Honors and The Popularity Poll

VERY EARLY IN ITS HISTORY, the American Hemerocallis Society recognized the need for an incentive program that would honor and encourage its members. There was also a growing need for a better means to evaluate the exploding market of daylilies. Through its Award & Honors system the first need has been admirably served. Questions have arisen from time to time as to the fulfillment of the second need.

It is not for want of trying that the effort to evaluate daylilies has sometimes broken down. Several dedicated committees have planned, experimented, lectured, and cajoled; yet undeserving daylilies manage to slip into positions of honor, both high and low, while worthy cultivars are ignored. The human element is a formidable hurdle. It even has been suggested that computers might do a better job. Unfortunately, they too prove to be inadequate tools when it comes to selecting daylilies. The problem is, they simply have no taste. Their choice usually leans toward the homeliest flower in the garden. Until something better comes along, gardeners will continue to rely on instinct—or the recommendations of Awards & Honors Judges, who frequently adopt the same approach.

The wonder is that such a large percentage of outstanding daylilies do make the important awards lists. This is a credit to some 600 Awards & Honors judges, a sufficient number of whom have good instincts, good collections from which to judge first-hand, and the integrity to ignore political persuasion.

IN THE BEGINNING

An excerpt from the 1964 revised edition of the *Judges' Handbook* reads as follows:

> The Awards & Honors program was initiated through the adoption of the amended Constitution and By-Laws of the Society on July 8, 1950, in Cleveland, Ohio. A provision was incorporated in this historic document to provide for the bestowal of appropriate awards and honors and for the establishment of an

Awards and Honors Committee to administer the program. Following the adoption of the new Constitution and By-Laws, the directors formulated a basic program which remained in effect, virtually unchanged, for ten years. The first A&H Committee was appointed at that time.

The program was originally designed to honor individual members and to recognize outstanding achievement in the field of hybridizing. The original authorization, therefore, provided for two basic honors and four classes of awards. In the first category, the Helen Field Fischer and the Bertrand Farr Medals were established. Then, in order to encourage the continuous development of improved new cultivars, the Stout Medal, the Award of Merit, the Honorable Mention, and the Junior Citation awards were also established. All of these awards and honors were officially bestowed for the first time in 1950 by the directors. In 1956, the President's Cup was added to the list of officially recognized awards and in 1961 the Donn Fischer Memorial Cup was also authorized.

— BERTIE FERRIS, *chairman*

THE POPULARITY POLL

Since this annual survey was originally made under the supervision of the Awards & Honors Committee, the Popularity Poll has usually been thought of as being a part of the Society's Awards & Honors program. In November 1963 the board established a separate Popularity Poll Committee to conduct this annual poll. It gave the general membership, not just the Awards & Honors Judges, the opportunity to state their favorites; thus the Poll is theoretically an indicator of popular appeal among a much larger group of growers. In fact, it hasn't turned out that way. Only about 30% of the members exercise their voting privileges.

Throughout most of AHS history, Popularity Poll balloting followed a fairly standard form. Ballots were tabulated and reported on a regional basis. Then regional results were consolidated by the Popularity Poll Committee and the top 100 cultivars were listed to form the Society's annual Popularity Poll. As an adjunct to the Poll, the David Hall Regional Trophy was established in 1961. By this means, members could identify cultivars which were ranked among the top by members in their own regions.

In 1988 the board of directors started to tamper with the Poll. They were dissatisfied with the low representation of voters. A weighted poll was tried, but that quickly proved to be vulnerable to manipulation. Then the nationally merged list was dropped in favor of simple regional tabulation. A narrow majority of the board thought that growers would find the regional lists more useful. However, where one purpose was served, another failed. The AHS no longer had a list that was appropriate for release to the general gardening public. Thus, in 1993, a new committee was formed for the purpose of devising an expanded national Popularity Poll that would take into account color and other flower and plant characteristics. A proposal was presented to the board in October 1994. It failed to gain approval in its first draft, so it is back to the drawing board.

TRIALS AND TRIBULATIONS

Bertie Ferris continues:

At the directors' annual meeting in November 1957, a special committee was appointed to study the A&H program from all angles and to prepare a comprehensive set of practices and procedures, as for some time the need for a full and comprehensive analysis of the Society's Awards & Honors program had been apparent. It was widely felt that certain clarifications and improvements in the program should be made. This committee, chairman being D.R. McKeithan of Oklahoma, completely revised the Awards & Honors system. A full explanation of this revision was published in the *Hemerocallis Journal* (V.12, #3)

A further revision of the system was presented to the board at the November 1960 board of directors meeting, by a special committee, of which Dr. Walter C. Hava was chairman. This report, with subsequent amendments, was adopted as the official program of the Society pertaining to Awards & Honors. From time to time, certain changes or additions may be made by the Awards Committee and approved by the board of directors, as was done at the November 1962 directors meeting.

The first revision, alluded to by Mrs. Ferris, included some strong new requirements that had at their root the object of upgrading the Awards &

Honors Judges themselves. The committee maintained the position that it is more important to stress the basic qualifications of the individual doing the judging than to hand down rigid rules for judges to follow. Tenure was out and reappointment was in, a system that wound the applicant through a maze of prescribed personages every two years.

Several judges took the new program as a personal affront. In 1959 John Lambert offered a constructive alternative:

> Recent changes in the procedure to select Awards & Honors Judges have, apparently, been based on the assumption that the only way to get better judgments is to get better judges. The proposals that follow rest upon a different set of assumptions. Specifically, it is assumed that bad judgments arise as often from inadequate judicial procedures as from inadequate judges and that a more clearly defined procedure for the nomination and selection of the clones to be honored will produce better judgments—regardless of the system used to select the judges themselves—than has hitherto been the case.
>
> Briefly, the Society needs an open-and-above-board procedure for the *nomination* of new clones for the Honorable Mention and, most especially, for the Junior Citation awards. In the past, accredited judges have never really known, in any *formal* way, what new hybrids were up for consideration. Technically, all are; actually, only a few are given serious attention and these few are promoted either by favored hybridizers or by a coterie of the favored hybridizers' friends. In this process worthy clones are sometimes overlooked, simply because no organized group is promoting them. On some occasions, less conscientious judges have been known to reach their decisions by connivance, barter, or worse. In brief, the judicial process permits, at best, and promotes, at worst, bad judging; to continue the present procedure will *not* guarantee better judging, regardless of the qualifications that may be set up for the selection of those who are to judge.

Dr. Lambert goes on to lay out a detailed nomination procedure with a suggested standard nomination blank. A modified version of the nomination system was put in place for the Honorable Mention award. Hybridizer nominations are today the basis of the HM list that is a part of the A&H Ballot.

The Junior Citation, on the other hand, continues to suffer from all the potential ailments cited by Dr. Lambert in his critique of the "judicial procedures." Some attempts have been made to verbalize its insignificance; others to wipe it out altogether. But to date it has survived all eradication efforts, mainly by the strength of its popularity with many hybridizers who find it an attractive selling point.

SPECIAL AWARDS

Since Bertie Ferris's 1964 report, several special annual awards have been authorized by the board. These are often funded as memorials and bear the name of the deceased. Some were installed for a specified period and have since been discontinued. All are listed below in the order of their appearance:

1964   ANNIE T. GILES AWARD—For the most outstanding small flower.

1970   LENINGTON ALL-AMERICAN AWARD—For a cultivar that performs outstandingly in most parts of the country. (Voted by the board of directors.)

1970   MILDRED SCHLUMPF AWARD—Until 1993, and before the death of Mildred Schlumpf, this photography award bore her husband's name: Robert Way Schlumpf Award - For the best color slide in each of two categories: single bloom and landscape. Winners chosen by committee.

1974   FLORIDA SUNSHINE CUP—For the best miniature or small-flowered cultivar displayed in a convention tour garden. (Voted by convention attendants.)

1974–   ROBERT P. MILLER MEMORIAL AWARD—For
1983   the best near-white daylily.

1974–   RICHARD C. PECK MEMORIAL AWARD—For
1983   the best tetraploid daylily.

1975   IDA MUNSON AWARD—For the most outstanding double flower.

1975   A.D. ROQUEMORE MEMORIAL AWARD—Photography award for the best slide of a daylily clump.

1976   NEWSLETTER AWARD—To the editor of the best regional newsletter.

1979   L. ERNEST PLOUF CONSISTENTLY VERY FRAGRANT DAYLILY AWARD—What more can be said except that it must be dormant.

1979   REGION 14 SEQUENCE AWARD—Photography award for the best color slides of a sequence of events involving daylilies.

1981–1990   JAMES E. MARSH AWARD—Given for the best purple or lavender daylily.

1985   DON C. STEVENS AWARD—For the outstanding eyed or banded daylily. Ten-year period of funding by donor club expires at the end of 1995.

1986   LAZARUS MEMORIAL PHOTOGRAPHY AWARD—For the best video recording of a presentation relating to daylilies.

1989   HARRIS OLSON SPIDER AWARD—For the best Spider or Spider-Variant.

1991   EUGENE S. FOSTER AWARD—For outstanding late-blooming cultivars.

The Stout Silver Medal

TOUT MEDAL WINNERS are cream risen to the top. A sifting procedure assures a top-quality daylily for a broad section of the country. Some members have been piqued by a system that would award the most prestigious cultivar medal to a daylily not adaptable to *all* parts of the country. Unfortunately, many *Hemerocallis* cultivars still show regional preferences although progress has been made in that area.

More likely, the true bone of contention is that the south has risen again. At one time, the strong corps of tetraploid breeders in the Chicago area held sway. Now, there are more Garden Judges in the south, more southern cultivars being bred, and more southern cultivars being sold to northern gardeners. A recent study indicates that more northern judges are voting for more southern daylilies than the reverse. Until allowable quotas for judgeships are filled in northern regions, the imbalance will remain. Thus, a preponderance of tender evergreens may show up on the Stout Medal list.

Gardeners have benefited from work being done by a few hybridizers—on both sides of the line—to breed a plant for everyone. The potential exists; but when it involves limiting other desirable traits, many hybridizers prefer to please part of the people all of the time.

Historical records indicate that this is not a new problem. In the 1968 *Yearbook*, Elmer Claar of Illinois expounds on regional daylilies and adaptability:

It is reported that HESPERUS and REVOLUTE do not do well in Florida, and certainly HIGH NOON, NARANJA, and RUFFLED PINAFORE have not done well in my garden. These five plants have each received the Stout Award, the highest honor given by the American Hemerocallis Society. PLAYBOY won the President's Cup in Florida at the 1960 Convention [and later the Stout Medal]. It was lovely in Florida, but it died in at least four gardens in the Chicago area in the winter of 1960. I lost two plants—one two years old; one only one year old. On the other hand, I have since grown Florida and California hybridized daylilies that have done as well as any that came from the North.

Adaptability is not the same as winter hardiness. It not only concerns temperature, cold and hot, but water, lack of water, humidity, air circulation or lack of it; that is, air pockets—all this as modified by the type of soil the plant is growing in—and its neighbors. Are the neighbors a protective aid, or do they use much of the food and water which the flower plant needs? Therefore, similar flowers may vary from year to year in the same garden. Two similar plants in the same garden but in different locations may differ, and flowers themselves differ during the varying hours of the day.

—ELMER CLAAR

No daylily is fail-safe. Not even a Stout Medal winner. Not even STELLA DE ORO.

Stout Silver Medal Winners 1950–1995

THE FOLLOWING PORTFOLIO includes all Stout Medal winners since the award was inaugurated in 1950, up to but not including the Golden Anniversary year. Date given in the caption refers to year in which the cultivar won the Stout Medal. Other information is from the Check List. The first registrations did not include flower size.

Stout Medal collections exist in both public and private gardens throughout the United States. Such collections, when accessible, allow daylily aficionados to study the progress that has been made by hybridizers over a relatively short time.

Pictures can't tell the whole story, but this easy stroll through the pages of history should reveal the more important trends and the extent of their development since the early 1950s.

photo by Frances Gatlin

3-2.
Partial view of the Stout Medal bed at the Missouri Botanical Gardens in St. Louis. Pink daylily in the foreground is SATIN GLASS.

AMERICAN HEMEROCALLIS SOCIETY MEDALS

Medals sponsored by the AHS bear the Society logo on one face and the name of the award and winner on the reverse. The Stout Silver Medal is one of four large medals awarded. Three of the awards, though established in 1950, had no "metal" to back them up until 1961 when funds became available. The daylily depicted on the face is 'Green Valley,' a 1959 registration by Hubert Fischer. This daylily is also pictured on the front cover of the *1968 Daylily Handbook* published by the American Horticultural Society, although it is captioned 'Buried Treasure.' An errata slip informs the reader that the front and back cover photos were reversed in this otherwise exemplary publication.

3-3. *HESPERUS (Hans P. Sass) S.M.-1950. Dormant, diploid, MLa, 42–48 in. tall.*

3-4. *PAINTED LADY (Hugh M. Russell) S.M.-1951. Evergreen, diploid, MRe, 36 in. tall.*

3-5. *POTENTATE, towering in rainy 1993. Most early hybrids were comparatively taller.*

KEY TO ABBREVIATIONS—
S.M.=Stout Silver Medal (date=year awarded) EE=extra early; E=early; EM=early midseason; M=midseason; MLa=midseason late; La=late; Re=recurrent bloom

3-6. *POTENTATE (Elizabeth Nesmith) S.M.-1952. Dormant, diploid, MRe, 42 in. tall.*

photo by Oscie Whatley

3-7. REVOLUTE *(Hans P. Sass)* S.M.-1953. *Dormant, diploid, MLaRe, 48 in. tall.*

photo by Frances Gatlin

3-8. DAUNTLESS *(Arlow Burdette Stout)* S.M.-1954. *Semi-ev, diploid, EMRe, 30–36 in. tall.*

photo by Oscie Whatley

3-9. PRIMA DONNA *(Ophelia Taylor)* S.M.-1955. *Evergreen, diploid, MRe, 36 in. tall.*

3-10. *NARANJA (Ralph Wheeler) S.M.-1956. Evergreen, diploid, MRe, 36 in. tall.*

3-11. *RUFFLED PINAFORE (Carl Milliken) S.M.-1957. Evergreen, diploid, M, 30 in. tall.*

3-12. *HIGH NOON (Carl Milliken) S.M.-1958. Evergreen, diploid, MRe, 36 in. tall.*

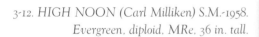

photo by Frances Gatlin

photo by Oscie Whatley

photo by Oscie Whatley

3-13. SALMON SHEEN (*Ophelia Taylor*) S.M.-1959. *Evergreen, diploid, ERe, 34 in. tall.*

3-14. FAIRY WINGS (*Mary Lester*) S.M.-1960. *Dormant, diploid, EM, 36 in. tall.*

3-15. PLAYBOY (*Ralph Wheeler*) S.M.-1961. *Evergreen, diploid, EM, 30 in. tall.*

3-16. BESS ROSS (*Elmer Claar*) S.M.-1962. *Diploid, M, 36 in. tall.*

3-17. MULTNOMAH *(Ezra Kraus)* S.M.-1963. *Dormant, diploid, M–MLa, 24 in. tall.*

3-18. FRANCES FAY *(Orville Fay)* S.M.-1964. *Dormant, diploid, EMRe, 24 in. tall.*

3-19. LUXURY LACE *(Edna Spalding)* S.M.-1965. *Dormant, diploid, MRe, 32 in. tall.*

3-20. CARTWHEELS *(Orville Fay)* S.M.-1966. *Dormant, diploid, M–MLa, 30 in. tall.*

3-21. *FULL REWARD (F. A. McVicker) S.M.-1967. Dormant, diploid, EM, 34 in. tall.*

3-22. *SATIN GLASS (Orville Fay) S.M.-1968. Dormant, diploid, M, 34 in. tall.*

3-23. *MAY HALL (David Hall) S.M.-1969. Dormant, diploid, EM, 26 in. tall.*

3-24. *AVA MICHELLE (Wilmer Flory) S.M.-1970. Semi-ev, diploid, MLa, 18 in. tall.*

3-25. *RENEE (William J. Dill) S.M.-1971. Dormant, diploid, M, 34 in. tall.*

3-26. *HORTENSIA (Charles E. Branch) S.M.-1972. Dormant, diploid, MRe, 34 in. tall, 5 in. dia. flower.*

3-27. *LAVENDER FLIGHT (Edna Spalding) S.M.-1973. Semi-ev, diploid, EM, 36 in. tall, 6¼ dia. flower.*

3-28. *WINNING WAYS (Allen J. Wild) S.M.-1974. Dormant, diploid, EM, 32 in. tall, 6 dia. flower.*

photo by Frances Gatlin

photo by Frances Gatlin

3-29. CLARENCE SIMON (W.B. MacMillan) S.M.-1975. *Evergreen, diploid, MRe, 8 in. tall, 6 in. dia. flower.*

3-30. GREEN FLUTTER (Lucille Williamson) S.M.-1976. *Semi-ev, diploid, LaRe, 20 in. tall, 3 in. dia. flower.*

photo by Oscie Whatley

photo by Frances Gatlin

3-31. GREEN GLITTER (Mattie C. Harrison) S.M.-1977. *Semi-ev, diploid, EMRe, 32 in. tall., 7 in. dia. flower.*

3-32. MARY TODD (Orville Fay) S.M.-1978. *Semi-ev, tet, E, 26 in. tall, 6 in. dia. flower.*

3-33. MOMENT OF TRUTH (W.B. MacMillan)
S.M.-1979. Diploid, MRe, 23 in. tall, 6-in. dia. flower.

photo by Oscie Whatley

3-34. BERTIE FERRIS* (Ury G. Winniford) S.M.-1980.
Dormant, diploid, E, 20 in. tall, 2½ in. dia. flower.

photo by Frances Gatlin

*First miniature to win the Stout Medal

3-35. ED MURRAY
(Edward T. Grovatt) S.M.-1981
Dormant, diploid, M, 30 in. tall,
4 in. dia. flower.

photo by Frances Gatlin

photo by Frances Gatlin

3-36. RUFFLED APRICOT (S. Houston Baker) S.M.-1982. Dormant, tet, EM, 28 in. tall, 7 in. dia. flower.

photo by Oscie Whatley

photo by Frances Gatlin

3-37. SABIE (W.B. MacMillan) S.M.-1983. Evergreen, diploid, ERe, 24 in. tall, 6 in. dia. flower.

3-38. MY BELLE (Kenneth G. Durio) S.M.-1984. Evergreen, diploid, ERe, 26 in. tall, 6½ in. dia. flower.

3-39. STELLA DE ORO (Walter Jablonski) S.M.-1985 Dormant, diploid, EMRe, 11 in. tall, 2¾ in. dia. flower.

3-40. JANET GAYLE (Lucille Guidry) S.M.-1986. Evergreen, diploid, ERe, 26 in. tall, 6½ in. dia. flower.

3-41. BECKY LYNN
(Lucille Guidry) S.M.-1987.
Semi-ev, diploid, EERe, 20 in. tall,
6¾ in. dia. flower.

photo by Harvey Horne

3-42. MARTHA ADAMS (Elsie Spalding) S.M.-1988. Evergreen,
diploid, EM, 19 in. tall, 6¾ in. dia. flower.

photo by Frances Gatlin

photo by Harvey Horne

3-43. BROCADED GOWN (Bryant Millikan)
S.M.-1989. Semi-ev, diploid, EMRe, 26 in. tall,
6 in. dia. flower.

3-44. FAIRY TALE PINK *(Charles F. Pierce)* S.M.-1990.
Semi-ev, diploid, MRe, 24 in. tall, 5½ in. dia. flower.

photo by Frances Gatlin

photo by Frances Gatlin

3-45. BETTY WOODS *(David Kirchhoff)* S.M.-1991.
Diploid double, ERe, 26 in. tall, 5½ in. dia. flower.

3-46. BARBARA MITCHELL
(Charles F. Pierce) S.M.-1992.
Semi-ev, diploid, MRe, 20 in. tall,
6 in. dia. flower.

photo by Frances Gatlin

3-47. *SILOAM DOUBLE CLASSIC*
(Pauline Henry) S.M.-1993.
Dormant, diploid double, EM, 16 in. tall,
5 in. dia. flower.

photo by Frances Gatlin

3-48. *JANICE BROWN (Edwin C. Brown)*
S.M.-1994. Semi-ev, diploid, EM, 21 in. tall,
4¼ in. dia. flower.

photo by Frances Gatlin

photo by Frances Gatlin

3-49. *NEAL BERREY (Sarah Sikes)*
S.M.-1995. Semi-ev, diploid, M, 18 in.
tall, 5 in. dia. flower.

Personal Awards

 OT ALL THE HIGH HONORS go to day-lilies. As a part of the same master plan that conceived the Stout Silver Medal Award, the Helen Field Fischer Gold Medal became a cherished symbol of meritorious service to the Society. Fittingly, the first medal was awarded to Helen Field Fischer herself, for her role in assembling the first daylily meeting at Shenandoah as well as for her enthusiastic championing of the daylily in her radio broadcasts. She also supervised the first AHS test garden. The Henry Field Nursery donated the plot, sprinkler system, and maintenance. Mrs. Fischer's meticulous observations are reported in the early *Journals*. (See p. 28.)

As an interesting sidelight on the contributions of the Fischer family, one of the early publications reveals that they not only produced the first *Yearbook* editor (Gretchen Harshbarger), but furthermore advanced the funds for the *Yearbook* itself.

Generosity was a family trait. Brother Henry had a refreshing if fatal attitude about money. It was kept in a community pot, and extended family members were free to dip in whenever a need arose.

HELEN FIELD FISCHER MEDAL

This medal is the Society's highest personal award, given as official recognition of distinguished and meritorious service rendered the Society by one of its members.

Helen Field Fischer	Iowa	1950
M. Frederick Stuntz	New York	1951
Viola Richards	Indiana	1952
Gretchen Harshbarger	Iowa	1953
Bess Ross	Iowa	1954
George E. Lenington	Missouri	1955
F. Edgar Rice	Oklahoma	1956
Hugh M. Russell	Texas	1957
Elmer A. Claar	Illinois	1958
Wilmer B. Flory	Indiana	1959
Maria Marcue	Iowa	1960
D. R. McKeithan	Oklahoma	1961
Frances Lamb	Kentucky	1962
Ophelia Taylor	Florida	1963
Hubert A. Fischer	Illinois	1964

Olive Hindman	Florida	1965
Lula Mae Purnell	Texas	1966
Ben Parry	Tennessee	1967
William E. Monroe	Louisiana	1968
George M. Darrow	Maryland	1969
Bertie Ferris	Texas	1970
Hyta Mederer	Georgia	1970
Walter C. Hava	Mississippi	1971
Molly Wheeler	Illinois	1972
Ethel Smith	Mississippi	1973
George T. Pettus	Missouri	1974
Willard Gardner	North Carolina	1975
Louise Simon	Louisiana	1975
Edna Lankart	Texas	1976
Ruth Mannoni	Kansas	1977
Betty Barnes	Mississippi	1978
Luther J. Cooper, Jr.	North Carolina	1979
Martha B. Hadley	Missouri	1980
Shirley Gene Wild	Missouri	1980
Daisy L. Ferrick	Kansas	1981
Olive Langdon	Alabama	1982
Mildred Schlumpf	Texas	1983
Lucia Bjorkman	Texas	1984
Luke Senior, Jr.	Arkansas	1985
Sarah Sikes	Alabama	1986
Ida Munson	Florida	1987
Betty Woods	Georgia	1988
Mavis G. Smith	Missouri	1989
Virginia Peck	Tennessee	1990
Selma Timmons	Georgia	1991
R. W. Munson, Jr.	Florida	1991
Clarence J. Crochet	Louisiana	1992
Frances Gatlin	Missouri	1993
Elly Launius	Mississippi	1993
Dorothea Boldt	Louisiana	1994
Bob Brooks	California	1995

REGIONAL SERVICE AWARDS

Several awards are given to recognize service at the regional level. The AHS has its own award for this purpose, voted by the board, based upon nominations from the membership. Regions can and do optionally create their own service awards for which they establish their own preferred guidelines.

Chapter 4
Making Publications

*This is the best book ever written by any
man on the wrong side of a question of
which he is profoundly ignorant.*
MACAULAY

The Journal

THE AMERICAN HEMEROCALLIS SOCIETY'S primary publication has flown under an assortment of banners, but since 1955 it has been affectionately dubbed "The Journal." In the circle of AHS, *Journal* can mean only one thing.

Historically, the word has been capitalized in AHS literature, even when it stands alone. Whether this is strict usage or strictly vanity, is a matter for debate among those who care about such things, but it is a tradition that will not be broken here.

THE YEARBOOKS

The first major publication was one of a series of annual *Yearbooks*, begun by AHS's parent organization, the Midwest Hemerocallis Society, and continued two years later as the American Hemerocallis Society *Yearbook*.

The *Yearbooks* were ambitious undertakings for so young an organization. They were released in

4-1. The first HEMEROCALLIS YEARBOOK, *published by the Midwest Hemerocallis Society in 1947. Edited by Gertrude Harshbarger.*

early summer, just in time to stimulate garden activity. As a rule, each issue exceeded 200 pages and was packed with a wealth of no-frills, meaty information. Owing to the number of pages, the bind started as a plastic coil, similar to the type used on some of the combined *Check Lists*. Later books were made with flat spines, known in the trade as "perfect binding."

The first *Yearbook*, published in 1947, bore the simple title *Hemerocallis* on the cover; but inside, on the title page, it was expanded to read: "The First Yearbook of The Midwest Hemerocallis Society." It was edited by Gretchen Harshbarger, talented daughter of Frederick and Helen Field Fischer.

Anyone in publishing would appreciate the challenge met by Editor Harshbarger. She assembled the *Yearbook* on one month's notice, supplying photographs, drawing the cover design, and drawing the original pen and ink sketch inside showing parts of a daylily. (A later fine interpretation by North Carolina artist Cheryl Postlewait graces the *Judging Daylilies* handbook.)

Mrs. Harshbarger may have had no electronic marvel on her desktop, but she had an irrefutable knack for inspiring cooperation in high places. The quality and quantity of contributions made the first *Yearbook* a collector's item. Her diversified skills did not go unnoticed. She went on to become a professional garden editor of *Household Magazine*.

The first *Yearbooks* were black and white with some duotone cover designs. Four-color was yet a distant dream. However, the inside pages featured many excellent halftone photos. Nowadays, the photographer with black and white film in the camera is an exception. Instead, slides are converted or grayscale scans are made from color prints. Neither method produces the best quality halftones. Cameras themselves are different too; though handier, they sometimes compromise quality.

"People pictures" were a staple of the *Yearbooks* and early *Journals*. These days, readers send mixed messages. Some want to see only daylilies, while others enjoy pairing names with faces. (This book is, without apology, people-oriented.)

AHS NEWSLETTERS

Although the *Yearbooks* were published only annually, members received three small newsletters in the off-season to round out the volumes. The first editions were truly small—a single sheet, printed on both sides. But soon the format expanded to eight legal-sized pages on no-nonsense yellow paper. This design continued until 1955 when *The Hemerocallis Society Newsletter* name was dropped in favor of *The Hemerocallis Journal*.

A division of labor marked some of the early publications. One editor might be assigned the *Yearbook* and another the newsletters.

THE HEMEROCALLIS JOURNAL

The assumption of the title *Hemerocallis Journal* for all four issues of the Society's publication was a matter of expediency, brought on by the need to comply with Second Class postal regulations. At the same time, a "permanent" editor was installed. This was Peggy Schultz from Minnesota who served for three years. She received a small stipend for her efforts.

The former Newsletters were slicked up a bit—now of *Journal* dimensions, printed on enamel paper, and fattened up to 16 pages. Black and white photos were included, inside and out. The Society still kept its one large yearbook issue, the only difference being that the original title was supplanted to a subhead position.

Finding and keeping qualified editors continued to be a problem. In 1966 the board of directors faced up to the challenge. President Richard Peck reports:

As you know, our editor, Wilmer Flory, has wished to relinquish his duties for some time. . . . Although I mentioned Wilmer's impending retirement in the Winter 1965 Journal, there has been a marvelous lack of applicants for the post. Not only have no volunteers presented themselves, but those likely individuals who were approached have been reluctant even to discuss the matter except to say no rather pointedly. After considering the problem for some

4-2. *An early* HEMEROCALLIS SOCIETY NEWSLETTER, *not to be confused with the regional newsletters of today. Most were 8 pages long. The three issues were designed to supplement the annual* YEARBOOKS.

4-4. *The first* HEMEROCALLIS SOCIETY YEARBOOK, *published after the Society's name change. Edited by Virginia Buterbaugh in 1949. Editors were unpaid then, so appointments turned over rapidly.*

4-5. *The first* Hemerocallis Journal, Yearbook Issue. *The name was changed to bring all four issues under the same title and thus effect a savings at the post office. This 1956 issue corresponded with the engagement of a "permanent" editor. (Color arrangement featured CRIMSON GLORY by charter member Carl Carpenter.)*

4-6. *The* Journal *as it appeared after the* Yearbooks *were phased out in 1971 and all four issues became comparable in content and format. The Winter 1980-81 issue pictured here is the last done by editor Ben Parry. The daylily is CINDY MARIE by Ken Durio.*

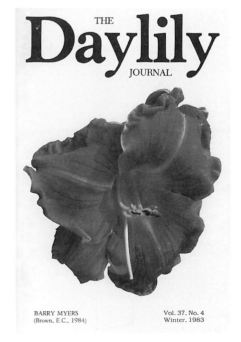

4-7. *The* Journal *gets a new name and new design by Ned Irish. This winter 1983 issue was edited by John Allgood and featured BARRY MYERS by E.C. Brown. The success of the cutout design was heavily dependent upon the photography and flower. When it was good, it was very, very good; and when it was bad . . .*

time and agreeing that we may never be able to pay what the work is worth, the Board decided to diminish somewhat the gap between the dedication necessary to do the work and the stipend paid for it so that the post might become less unattractive to the talent the Society undoubtedly harbors. At all events, the salary of both the editor and secretary by Board action will be $2,400 annually beginning in 1966.

This powerful inducement—or more likely it was altruism on her part—snared Ben Parry, AHS's longest-serving editor to date. She was to be awarded the Helen Field Fischer medal during this term.

As for the long-suffering Wilmer Flory, cited in Dr. Peck's "President's Message," poor Wilmer would not realize his dream of retirement for another 12 months. He had already put in several years of hardline duty in various national offices before he was tapped for his five-year stint as editor. Eventually, he was called into service again as AHS president.

Long-term editors have been the exception. During Ben Parry's 14 years, the *Journal* achieved some stability. In 1968 the extra-fat, perfect-bound issue was absorbed into four nominally equal, saddle-stitched issues, running to about 72 pages each. Along with that reduced "yearbook" issue came a one-time treasure, the *Daylily Handbook*, published by the American Horticultural Society in cooperation with the AHS. (More about that publication later.) The larger summer yearbook issue was revived in 1969 and 1970. In 1971 it was gone for good, although all four issues have gradually increased in size over the years. Further changes in the overall format were limited to occasional splashes of color until Mrs. Parry's retirement at the end of 1980.

THE DAYLILY JOURNAL

The year 1981 heralded a new design, a new editor, and a new name. The board sought a more modern look for the Society's publication. Already, color had been introduced.

The change of name to *The Daylily Journal* was a bold stroke, not universally applauded. However, the board considered the botanical term *Hemerocallis* to be a distancing factor between the AHS and general gardening public. The switch to "Daylily" brought instant name recognition. At least the Society was less of an enigma to curious mail carriers.

4-8. *Modification of the Ned Irish cover design of the* Daylily Journal. *Fall 1989 issue featuring Mort Morss's FANTASY FINISH. Edited by Frances Gatlin.*

Member artist Ned Irish designed a clean, uncluttered, contemporary cover to carry the new title, with emphasis on the word "daylily" and a single flower cutout imposed upon a stark white background. The masthead is still in use today, but the flower cutout, which gave the design its clean look, hit a snag. The cover positions are often sold to hybridizers and the hybridizers did not like their blooms displayed in this way. So back in went the natural backgrounds. With this modification, the design still stands today.

Editor John Allgood entered the scene as the above changes were being put in place. He introduced a more lavishly designed *Journal*, more color, and supporting artwork contributed by Steve Baldwin and Phil Reilly. The membership grew.

In 1985, John Allgood resigned and a relatively new member, Roger Mercer from North Carolina, was hired as a replacement. This proved to be a short-lived solution, for scheduling difficulties brought Mr. Mercer's term to a close at the end of 18 months. His five *Journals* were in the attractive "designed" vein begun by John Allgood although the front cover was temporarily modified to accommodate on-site printing limitations. Additional color was supported through the use of hybridizer-subsidized articles and a large contribution from the Greater Atlanta Hemerocallis Society. The *Journal* schedule, however, fell behind.

The year 1987 was a year of chaos for the *Journals*. A retiring editor, an interim editor, and a new editor were employed within a 12-month period. In a classic case of "more is less," the *Journal*, Volume #41 had only three issues.

Frances Gatlin was hired in June 1987 to produce a fall issue that would be mailed in August. In her haste to get to press, the new editor imprinted the wrong volume number on the front cover—Volume 41 instead of Volume 40. Inexperience breeds imaginative solutions, and this editor chose to pick up and carry forward, leaving Volume 40 to disappear into the dust—much to the consternation of librarians all over the country!

The *Journals* were back on schedule, and AHS began to regroup. The experience of 1987 had left some scars. A devastating drop in membership took many months to reverse itself. However, once the recovery was complete, growth accelerated far beyond the precipice of that troubled year.

As for the "missing" Volume 40, let this record forever stand to excuse the concurrence of Volume 51 with the AHS 50th Anniversary.

4-9.

ENTER COMPUTERS

It was the desire of the board of directors to take advantage of a new industry that sprang up in 1986. "Desktop publishing" promised more control and economic advantages over traditional typesetting and layout. With this object in mind, Chicagoland Daylily Society donated the funds to purchase one of the first Apple LaserWriters®. It was a notably generous contribution, for in those days the Laser-Writer® carried a list price of over $5000. Other local societies followed suit with donations for specific equipment and the DTP ship was launched.

Following the fall issue of 1987, all subsequent *Journals* have been produced as camera-ready copy in a home-office environment. It is a system that has served the Society well. While rapid obsolescence inherent in the computer industry has somewhat eroded expected savings, better control of copy and scheduling has more than justified the changeover.

COLOR IN THE JOURNAL

It began subtly, with duotones on the covers of early *Yearbooks*. The first four-color appeared on the front cover of the 1956 *Yearbook* issue. Color made a one-time lavish display in the 1960 *Yearbook*, when the Wild's of Sarcoxie, Missouri, donated 16 pages in full color. It slipped into the inside pages during Ben Parry's long reign. It picked up steam with John Allgood at the helm and continued though Roger Mercer's shorter term. In more recent years, by popular demand, it has become an every-issue event.

A sampling of the last survey, conducted in 1993, indicates that more color is at the top of many members' want lists. Several local clubs, regions, and even individuals have backed up their requests with generous donations.

At this writing, four-color is still very expensive. When computer technology advances to the extent that desktop separations are completely satisfactory and can be executed with some degree of automation, the AHS will probably invest in equipment for that purpose. At this time, high-end drum scanners represent a much greater investment than the purchase price of the original LaserWriter.

Another consideration in doing desktop color is the time and skill involved. Perhaps the editor's office has reached the limit of diversification for a one-person operation. When typesetting and layout was added with the new desktop publishing responsibilities, all pretense of "part-time" was removed from the job description. However, experience has shown that when the welfare of the *Journal* is at stake, help is usually only a line of type away.

4-10. *Gretchen Harshbarger, editor of the Society's first* YEARBOOK. *She was a woman of many talents. With a degree in Landscape Architecture and skills in writing, art, and photography, she was well qualified to assume the position of Garden Editor for* HOUSEHOLD MAGAZINE. *The post led to her receiving the Asta Award for outstanding horticultural journalism.*

4-11. *Peggy Schultz, hired as "permanent" editor, served from 1956 until 1958.*

THROUGH THE YEARS—

Journal Editors

4.12. *Laura Gayer, served from the end of 1959 through 1960.*

4.13. *Edwin C. Munson of Illinois. No relation to the Munsons of Gainesville, Florida. Edited* YEARBOOKS *1953–1954.*

4-14. *Wilmer B. Flory, began a 5-year term in the 1961. Edited* YEARBOOKS *1961 through 1965.*

4-15. Ben Parry, as she began her term in 1966. She served for 14 years.

4-16. Barbara Mitchell, interim editor, early 1981.

4-17. John Allgood. Served as editor from 1981 through 1985.

photo by Harvey Horne

4-19. Frances Gatlin, current editor (1995). Began term in late 1987 when "desktop publishing" was adopted for the JOURNAL.

photo by Helen Davenport

4-18. Roger Mercer, editor from 1986 to spring of 1987.

photo by Harvey Horne

Photos not available for editors Virginia Buterbaugh (*Yearbook* 1949), and Mrs. Ernest Hardison, Jr., (1952-1955).

Other Society Publications

HEN THE SOCIETY was in its infancy, almost all of its records were printed in the #2 issue of the *Journal* (Yearbook). As records accumulated into significant masses of information, they were gradually removed and distributed in separate volumes or supplements.

THE CHECK LIST

Probably the most important "other publication" by the AHS is the *Check List*. The full impact of this responsibility will be covered more thoroughly in the chapter dealing with registrations. The few comments here will relate to publishing from an editor's viewpoint.

In the beginning, the annual registrations were included in the *Journal*. With breeder enthusiasm running every bit as high in those days, it was not long before other provisions had to be made. An annual supplement to the *Journal* was the answer. The practice is still followed today. The volume number corresponds to that of the *Journal*. The *Check List* is now an optional purchase.

It might be well to touch on the spelling of the title. One member recently complained that *checklist* is properly spelled as one word. Perhaps. It depends upon which dictionary one chooses to worship. Some contemporary dictionaries have come around to the single-word spelling. However, at the time AHS started making *Check Lists*, the combined spelling was not an option. The present editor has elected to maintain some consistency until proven hopelessly out of fashion. (Conversely, the Society has been quite trendy with *Journal* titles.)

A bona fide procedure for registering daylilies was in place before the AHS was organized. The American Plant Life Society, discussed below under the heading of its publication *Herbertia*, organized much of the material for what is now informally called the *Brown Check List*, covering the period from 1893 to 1957. When the American Hemerocallis Society was formed, the APLS Society turned over its records and cooperated in the publishing of the first *Check List*.

Since that time, all registrations have been published annually by the AHS. Periodic combined lists are produced when the separate annual records become too cumbersome to search. The first independent effort of AHS to produce a combined *Check List*—covering 25 years—was quite a challenge to finance. Life Membership packages were sold at bargain rates in order to have a fund to borrow against. Fortunately, the *Check List* now has its own self-supporting fund.

Possibly no other facet of the AHS records has benefited so greatly from computer technology. Since the *Check List* has been computerized, the registrar sends the data via computer diskette to the editor for final formatting. No retyping is necessary and as a consequence a likely occasion for errors has been eliminated. (In the olden days, one typesetter managed to misspell the name of a well-known hybridizer six different ways in a single volume!)

Another advantage to computerizing the registrations is the ease with which they can be merged for combining *Check Lists*.

Some members see yet another potential use: selling the computer diskettes. At this writing, a computerized *Check List* is not available. The prospect is viewed with equal parts enthusiasm and alarm. Anyone who is involved with computers can probably figure out why.

MEMBERSHIP ROSTER

The *Roster* was another "supplement" that came to be detached from the body of the *Journal*. Prior to 1971, it was included in the *Yearbook* issues. The discontinuance of the *Yearbook* as a special oversize issue necessitated making other provisions for the growing *Roster*.

Until 1989 the *Roster* was published annually. Now it is a biennial publication, enlarged with the membership to 144 independent pages. Optional telephone numbers extend its bulk. It is no longer a "supplement" of the *Daily Journal* since biennial publication interrupted its numbering ties.

The *Journal* editor has traditionally been responsible for the production while the executive

4-20. *Other AHS publications. Clockwise from upper left:* 1. *A combined* CHECK LIST—*produced at intervals dictated by volume of registrations.* 2. *Annual* CHECK LIST, *printed each spring, listing registrations of the previous year.* 3. ROSTER, *printed biennially.* 4. JUDGING DAYLILIES—*handbook for Exhibition and Garden Judges.* 5. *Three "mini-books." ("Growing Ideas" by columnist Mavis Smith).* 6. DAYLILIES, THE BEGINNER'S HANDBOOK, *1991 edition.*

secretary supplies the data. The *Roster*, like the *Check List*, benefited greatly from electronic transfer.

CUMULATIVE AWARDS & HONORS

The last data file to be removed from the *Journal* was that of the Cumulative Awards. However, it became an orphan for a time before receiving a permanent home of its own in 1991. For several years, a semi-cumulative list had been relegated to the annual *Check List Supplement*. This solution did not satisfy anybody involved, especially the registrar, who rightly claimed that the cost of printing awards should neither be charged against registrations, nor invade the space thereof.

It was a point well taken. A separate booklet available at nominal cost now lists all the awards since 1950.

HANDBOOK FOR JUDGES

The printing history of the first *Handbook for Judges* is reviewed in the chapter dealing with shows and exhibitions. The first edition goes back to 1955. The handbook is revised periodically as the need occurs.

Since the manual is a combined guide for Exhibition Judges and Garden Judges (formerly called Awards & Honors Judges), four committees are involved: Exhibitions, Exhibition Judges & Clinics, Awards & Honors, and Garden Judges & Workshops. Usually, an editor is chosen from one of these committees to oversee production of the book.

Earlier handbooks were formatted in the manner of thin *Journals*. That is, they were 6x9 inches with a staple-stitched bind. In 1990 the format was changed to a loose-leaf notebook for ease of revision. The new edition, edited and produced by Ken Cobb, received high marks for ease of use and attractiveness, not to mention the improvements made to the system. This 1990 book, entitled *Judging Daylilies*, was a big hit.

HELP FOR NEW GROWERS

The Society has published several different titles offering basic information for new growers.

Originally, a circular called *Daylilies for Every Garden* by Fosler & Kamp was included with new member packets. When this was no longer available,

William Vaughn was appointed to compile a pamphlet which came to be titled *The Beginner's Bulletin*. It contained cultural information for various parts of the country.

The most ambitious and generous project to benefit new members was the 1978 Beginner's Handbook, *Everything You've Always Wanted to Know About Daylilies*. It was a 72-page softbound booklet, edited by Ben Parry and John Allgood, and it was loaded with information. In an amazing demonstration of largesse, the board decided to include it as a bonus to all new members. However, this practice was later determined to be too costly. The book was continued as a popular sale item.

A smaller more modest pamphlet was designed for new-member packets. Printed in the form of a 16-page booklet under the title *The Wonderful World of Daylilies*, it contained helpful lists and basic cultural information. But this, too, proved to be too expensive since the lists had to be updated annually. Eventually, it was discontinued and the various lists are now dropped into new-member packets without ceremony.

Meanwhile, plans were afoot to update the popular *Beginner's Handbook* which had already enjoyed two reprints. The final printing of the original was coordinated by Ainie Busse and involved commissioning new artwork to replace that which was lost.

In 1991 an extensive revision was completed. It included color and many text changes. This new expanded edition, titled *Daylilies, The Beginner's Handbook*, was edited by Frances Gatlin and remains in print today.

THE "DEFINITIVE" BOOK BURNING

The publication that has come closest to being the definitive book on daylilies is a perfect-bound, soft cover volume printed in 1968 as a cooperative effort with the American Horticultural Society. Title: *Daylily Handbook*. The American Hemerocallis Society had originally planned it as an independent project, but when word leaked out, the American Horticultural Society approached the board with a proposal. They would assist with editing and print the issue as a special publication for their own subscribers as well as for AHS members. It was an arrangement that had worked well with other plant societies.

George M. Darrow coordinated and co-edited the book with Frederick G. Meyer from the American Horticultural Society. The writing was done by highly qualified AHS members, many of whom were active in related fields of science. Various writers covered technical subjects, practical gardening, history, and just about every aspect of daylilies and the Society up to that time. Thanks to AHS contributors, impressive color plates were included. All in all, it was a magnificent achievement.

Alas, disaster loomed. Shortly after the initial distribution, lightning ignited a fire in the log cabin where editor Ben Parry had stored the new books that were to be sold. By the time the family reached the site, the walls had collapsed. A few boxes were dragged from the ruins, but none of the 1,700 books escaped serious injury.

The disaster sent a challenge to the membership. At the request of Mrs. Parry, generous donations poured in. In relatively short order, the means became available to print 1,000 replacement copies.

Perhaps they should have held out for 2,000 copies. The book is now a collector's item. This editor counted herself fortunate to be able to purchase one of the charred copies. The pungent odor of scorch and mildew endure after 17 years, but the book is still a treasure.

HERBERTIA

Even though *Herbertia* does not fit under the heading of AHS publications, the early issues of this publication deserve special mention. Beginning in the 1930s, long before daylilies had the American Hemerocallis Society as a champion, the American Amaryllis Society took the *Hemerocallis* under its wing because of the close phylogenetic relationship to the *Amaryllis* family of plants. Hamilton P. Traub, distinguished plant scientist, published the society's yearbook, *Herbertia*, and many important later-to-be-AHS-members were regular contributors. Those volumes published by the original American Amaryllis Society detail some of the most important work done with *Hemerocallis* during that period.

Herbertia is still being published, although its organization is now the International Bulb Society (see page 108). As such, it is much more diversified and cannot devote the degree of attention to daylilies that characterized the original organization.

REGIONAL NEWSLETTERS

Although not nationally distributed, the AHS regional newsletters have provided a valuable link in the membership chain. They are published at the discretion of the various AHS regions, at intervals generally ranging from two to four issues per year. All AHS members are entitled to whatever newsletters may be printed in their own regions. Output is highly dependent upon resources and available talent. Since reimbursement from the national coffers amounts to but a token of the actual cost, regions often hold plant auctions to finance their newsletters. These publications which began as minimal mimeographed sheets have grown up to sometimes-elaborate, information-packed formats. Several newsletters now carry color photographs.

Newsletters are the cement that holds the regions together. For members who can't attend regional meetings because of failing health or job commitments, the newsletters provide an armchair overview. Regional garden tours and activities are covered in detail. Cultivar recommendations and gardening practices can be given more weight when they flow from the pen of a neighbor who has walked in the same brand of shoes. For some readers, the newsletters are the best part of an AHS membership.

MISCELLANY

The AHS issues small inexpensive, photocopied booklets on various subjects taken from articles that have appeared in the *Journal*. They are designed to fill membership requests for material on special topics. The "mini-books" continue to be popular.

The *Guidelines for Regional Vice Presidents and Regional Publicity Directors* now in use is a comprehensive document as edited by Dorothea Boldt with the assistance of Ken Cobb in 1990. A much more succinct guide was written by Edna Lankart and published in the March 1970 issue of *The Hemerocallis Journal*. A somewhat later, concise version edited by Clarence Crochet remained in place until 1990.

Other publications have been written and revised over the years to fill specific needs that relate to the necessary business of any organization. They are of interest primarily to those unfortunate few who were absent when the committees were appointed.

Chapter 5

Making Daylilies

The present soon becomes the past
With dawn, tomorrow is to-day.
Not long what now is best will last
Since man will find a better way.
EDGAR A. GUEST

Thirty-Eight Thousand & Counting

S AN INDISPENSABLE COG in the Society, hybridizers have no peer. That is not to say their circle is exclusive. So great is the lure of "making daylilies" that almost every AHS member has tried it at least once. The ease with which crosses can be made has invited amateurs to join professionals in producing over 38,000 registered cultivars, some of which represent breakthroughs in color, form, and other tangible improvements.

The number of hybridizers who have made significant contributions to the gene pool is greater than we could hope to list. For the selections that follow, we turn to the Society's most auspicious award for hybridizing. The featured hybridizers represent the complete list of Bertrand Farr Medal winners, from the inception of the award in 1950 through 1995.

Inevitably, the system has its failings. Astute readers will see obvious omissions. Who would not agree that Walter Jablonski made a landmark contribution in the field of hybridizing with his introduction of STELLA DE ORO? By the same token, not all Bertrand Farr winners are created equal.

Where credit seems to warrant fuller coverage we have expanded some listings into article form. Even so, these notes scarcely touch the contributions made by major breeders, many of whom were scientists who unlocked doors that allowed hundreds of pollen dabbers to enjoy the successes we see exhibited in today's lavish forms.

Special mention must be made of two turn-of-the-century Englishmen, George Yeld and Amos Perry. George Yeld, of course, named the first daylily hybrid, 'Apricot.' Both his and Amos Perry's developments were used by Stout and the limited pocket of hybridizers practicing in the United States during the '30s and '40s when serious breeding with the daylily commenced here. That Yeld and Perry do not fit in the biographical list to follow points up a weakness in our attempt to pigeonhole. Their story deserves telling and who better to do so than George Yeld himself. Writing in the foreword of Amos Perry's privately published diary, Yeld reveals something about himself and Perry, as well as the state of *Hemerocallis* early in this century.

(Dated Dec. 12, 1937, the excerpt is from the "Foreword" written by the late George Yeld for Amos Perry's Diary)

I began to hybridise the *Hemerocallis*, or Day Lily, at Clifton Cottage, York, in 1877. Its name is a falsehood, for instead of being "the beauty of a day," and therefore shortlived, it has so many successive blooms on a stem that its brilliance lasts for many days, and therefore it is comparatively longlived. The plants in

photo courtesy Sydney Eddison

5-1. *George Yeld, 1867–1917, Yorkshire schoolmaster and plantsman who produced the first known daylily hybrid, 'Apricot,' in 1893.*

the garden were all of the varieties flava and fulva. Those which I was able to acquire were *Middendorffii, Dumortierii* (syn *Sieboldi* and *rutilans*) from the York nurseries, and *graminea*, or *minor*, a little later from Messrs. Fisher, Son and Sibray, of Sheffield.

They tell me I am the first hybridist of this family, the flower being Apricot (A.M., 1893.)

The variety *aurantiaca major*, a chance importation from Japan, at first believed to be a species, but now recognised to be a hybrid, gained the F.C.C. in 1895. It is a glorious flower and has played much the same part among Day Lilies as Dominion and Alcazar did among Irises.

Mr. Amos Perry was much attracted by the Day Lilies, and devoted himself with skill, perseverance, and patience to the production of such fine flowers as E.A. Bowles, Flavia, Margaret Perry, Winnie Nightingale, and George Yeld, and with the arrival of *fulva rosea*, a wild Chinese variety, I've no doubt we shall see many new forms of a lighter or deeper red, and red is a colour which advertises itself. We may expect, too, a further extension of his well-known exhibits at the Royal Horticultural Society. Some idea of the advance of the genus in numbers may be gained from the fact that I began with less than half-a-dozen varieties in 1877, and that I now have upwards of 30 varieties of my own raising, while Mr. Perry, in his most interesting and informative catalogue, offers upwards of 100.

To those who begin to cultivate the *Hemerocallis* with the help of this catalogue (what would it not have been to me in 1877!) I will venture to suggest the following plants as a first selection:

I. Inexpensive: *flava, aurantiaca major*—Margaret Perry.
II. Somewhat more expensive: E. A. Bowles, G. Yeld, J. S. Gayner.
III. Americans: Mikado, Soudan, Theron.

The plant that is going to revolutionize the genus, *viz., fulva rosea*, is naturally costly, since the plants are so few. But the enthusiast, if I may speak for him, is glad to get it at any price. I may mention that my plant in its first year produced five stems, with satisfactory supply of seed pods.

Next summer I expect to see Mr. Perry's enthusiasm richly rewarded, and in two years' time I may greet a welcome brood of seedlings of my own.

—GEORGE YELD, from *Amos Perry's Diary*

5-2. *Amos Perry, an important English nurseryman and hybridizer of the early 1900s. He admired George Yeld's work and quickly recognized the advantage of making new daylily hybrids for his own nursery trade. Perry was the younger of the two men. He lived to become a member of the new Hemerocallis Society in America and to register several of his daylilies.*

ONE HUNDRED KINDS IN THE TRADE! (1934)

Sue Garman of Maryland contributed an original 1934 *Better Homes and Gardens* article in which the writer Fleeta Brownell Woodroffe states, "Amos Perry, in England, has produced a group of remarkable new hybrids in matchless combinations of rosy and fulvous colorings. . . ."

The beautifully phrased word pictures that follow could be describing near relatives of *H. fulva*. Ms. Woodroffe goes on to observe about daylilies of her era: "There are, counting the 12 recognized as species, more than 100 kinds now in the trade."

"I HAVE DAYLILIES BLOOMING" —WOODROFFE, *BH&G*

*5-3. Clifton Cottage,
York, England—
home of George Yeld.*

We have already mentioned the early American Plant Life Society whose members of the day included such notables as Arlow B. Stout, Ezra J. Kraus, and Elizabeth Nesmith. Much of their work predated the formation of the American Hemerocallis Society, as did certain registrations that were to be recognized with the Stout Medal.

The new Society dedicated its first *Yearbook* to Hans Peter Sass, "Our Great Midwest Hybridizer," but he did not live to receive his highest awards.

The Chicago Area Breeders were another established group that had already taken preliminary steps toward forming a national daylily society when word spread of the Midwest Hemerocallis Society's organization. Thenceforth, the Chicago group dropped their plans and became instead Charter Members of the Hemerocallis Society that had its origin in Shenandoah. Several of this group were active in the tetraploid movement that rocketed to new heights at the 1961 national convention in Chicago. Paul Watts provided biographical notes on members of this elite group, who are heavily represented on the list to follow.

5-4. Hans Peter Sass. With his brother Jacob and nephew Henry, he operated the world-famous Sass Gardens in Nebraska where he began breeding daylilies in 1918. Hans died in September of 1949 at the age of 81, never having received the Bertrand Farr award. However, his 1933 daylily HESPERUS was the winner of the first Stout Medal in 1950 and his REVOLUTE received the honor in 1953.

The Sass brothers were born in Germany where Hans began the study of botany. When he was sixteen his parents settled the family on a farm near Omaha. Both brothers and Jacob's son Henry had long careers in breeding many flowers—especially iris, peonies, and daylilies.

Hybridizers We Have Known

HE BERTRAND FARR MEDAL is a distinguished honor reserved for members who have attained outstanding results in the field of hybridizing. It is voted by the AHS Board of Directors, based on nominations by the membership. Established in 1950, the annual awards total 46 on the eve of the Golden Anniversary of the AHS. Winners appear below in chronological order.

ARLOW BURDETTE STOUT - 1950

For 47 years prior to his death in 1957 at the age of 81, Arlow Burdette Stout was interested in the collecting, study, and hybridizing of *Hemerocallis*. As a prodigious writer, he has given us firsthand accounts of hybridizing and other areas of research. The seeds of industry were planted early in life:

> I cherish many memories of home, school, and social life in the humble and wholesome setting of the rural community at Albion, Wisconsin. At an early age there were chores for me; then came light labor in the care of a vegetable garden, and my mother was

one of the best gardeners; and later there were long days of hard work on the farm. But in that community honest labor was dignified; it brought not only the necessities but the pleasures of life; it was the privilege of everyone except the unfortunates.

As a curious youth, he was puzzled to observe that two plants of the family garden that had the most conspicuous flowers did not produce capsules and seeds, viz., the old familiar fulvous daylily (*Hemerocallis fulva clone* Europa) and the tiger lily (*Lilium tigrinum*). Years later, when he came to the New York Botanical Garden, plants of these two clones were obtained for experimental study. His interest centered on reproduction in flowering plants with special reference to the conditions of sterility and fertility. Greg Piotrowski, NYBG gardener, describes the arduous path to overcoming apparent sterility in *Hemerocallis fulva*:

> By the year of 1926, the Stout experiments using *H. fulva* as a seed and pollen parent yielded 23 seed capsules from over 7000 attempts at cross pollination with other diploid daylilies, including many species.

5-5.
*Arlow Burdette Stout—
his daughter's favorite
photo of him.*

Of seed produced from the 23 capsules, only seven seeds germinated.

When these and other hybrid seedlings were in bloom, they were observed by several daylily growers. These daylily enthusiasts encouraged Dr. Stout to continue hybridizing since many of the seedlings were superior to daylilies that were available at the time. Dr. Stout also observed that his seedlings had horticultural value, and if possible should be introduced to the gardening public. But horticultural display was always secondary to Dr. Stout's scientific studies.

Because the New York Botanical Garden does not distribute plant material commercially, Dr. Stout made an arrangement with the Farr Nursery Company in Pennsylvania to propagate, grow, and sell named Stout cultivars as well as grow and evaluate seedlings. Divisions were to be priced no higher than $3.00. About one year after the agreement was made, Bertrand Farr, owner of the nursery, died; but the terms of the agreement were upheld by his successors. Later, when the American Hemerocallis Society established its highest award for hybridizing, it was named after Bertrand Farr and the first of these annual awards went to Arlow Burdette Stout.

Greg Piotrowski continues:

It is evident from many of the cultivars Stout introduced, that *H. fulva* was involved with a great number of them. These cultivars resulted from his sterility experiments with that species. Working with *H. fulva* and *H. fulva* varieties and cultivars was slow because of the sterility problems. Results often were slow in coming; in some cases breeding programs went on for 20 years or longer. . . .

Much work was also done with miniature daylilies. Using *H. multiflora* as a basis for this program, Dr. Stout used other species to achieve colors other than the yellow of *H. multiflora* in a miniature-flowered daylily. . . .

Another species that Dr. Stout often worked with was *H. altissima*, the "Tall Daylily." The original plants of *H. altissima* and *H. multiflora* were sent to him from China by Dr. A. Steward, director of Nanking University. *Hemerocallis altissima* grows to seven feet and is nocturnal (night blooming), not much value to most gardeners. However, Dr. Stout saw value in having a tall, day-blooming daylily. He began cross-

pollinating this daylily with others to obtain new colors and achieve a diurnal (day blooming) flowering habit.

Current nursery catalogs still advertise the altissima strain of daylilies. These plants are over forty years old and are little known by most gardeners. Some of the "altissima cultivars" still available are *H.* 'Challenger' and *H.* 'Autumn Minaret.'

A valuable habit that both *H. altissima* and *H. multiflora* have is a late flowering season. Several cultivars were named and introduced which capitalize on lateness of bloom. The "August" and "Autumn" cultivars such as *H.* 'Autumn Prince' and *H.* 'August Orange' are two such daylilies. Other daylily species that Dr. Stout frequently used in his breeding programs were *H. aurantiaca* and *H. thunbergii*.

Some of Dr. Stout's cultivars (which were called clones during his time) are nothing more than the result of the cross-pollination of two or more species. But others, of course, are much more in-depth. For example, *H.* 'Theron,' the famous maroon-colored daylily [pictured on the dust jacket of the 1986 reissue of Dr. Stout's book *Daylilies*], took 25 years of work, crossing and recrossing, to achieve the final results. Other Stout cultivars are not hybrids at all but merely forms of the species that differed in some way from the typical form. Other distinct plants were named from seed selections of particular species. . . .

5-6. *Carl Milliken, California hybridizer who claimed two Stout Medals, back-to-back.*

Over 350 of Stout's papers have been printed in botanical journals and garden magazines. The most accessible of his writings today is the reprint of his 1934 *Daylilies: The Wild Species and Garden Clones, Both Old and New of the Genus Hemerocallis*. The 1986 reprint, edited by Darrel Apps, includes color plates that were commissioned by Stout for the book he was working on at the time of his death.

CARL MILLIKEN - 1951

California hybridizer Carl Milliken made his first introductions in 1948. He shares with Lucille Guidry the signal honor of being one of only two hybridizers to win a pair of Stout Medals back to back. These were for RUFFLED PINAFORE (1957) and HIGH NOON (1958). Nevertheless, it was GARNET ROBE, introduced in 1948 that brought Mr. Milliken more attention. For many years it was the highest-ranked red daylily on the Society's Popularity Poll. Author Philip Corliss of Arizona claimed to have been intimately acquainted with GARNET ROBE for 12 years when he characterized the daylily and its hybridizer with these words:

> It reached a diameter of six inches, making it probably the largest red daylily in total segment area up to that time [1948] and displayed a hitherto unsuspected yellow border on all petals and sepals. I have often told how Mr. Milliken tilted back in his swivel office chair and said, "You must have received the wrong plant—we'll send you another," and then added: "Garnet Robe with a yellow border! My, my, wouldn't that be something?"

Unlike RUFFLED PINAFORE which was a fine parent, GARNET ROBE proved to be difficult if not impossible to breed.

Carl Milliken was an accurate record keeper and until 1949, when health troubles interfered, all breeding records were faithfully transferred to the "stud books." However, some later records were lost and several errors were discovered among parentages listed in the *Check List*.

Enter Ben Hager and Sid DuBose of iris reknown. The two men literally uncovered the mystery of the missing parents. Making a careful search of the seedling bed, they found "a three-inch wooden label bearing the neat writing of Carl Milliken, still legible although it had been written in pencil and been buried fully five years!" More such labels were uncovered and by painstaking reconstruction the two men traced correct parentages for almost the entire line of Milliken daylilies. (A question remains about HIGH NOON, the 1958 Stout Medal winner.) The story, told by Ben Hager, and the listing of daylilies is recorded in the 1959 *Yearbook*.

MARY LESTER - 1952

Mary Lester of Atlanta was a charter member of AHS, but her daylily collection was started much earlier—in 1920. It began with the species. Her first cross was *H.* 'Aurantiaca Major' with pollen from *H. minor*. The result was a large pale yellow registered as EARLY BIRD. "Unfortunately," she says, "it was evergreen like its pod parent, and was only hardy in the Deep South."

After this excitement, she began collecting all the known hybrids in this country and a few from Amos Perry in England. (Imagine the time when one could think of collecting all the known hybrids!)

As a member of the American Plant Life Society, she received inspiration from such pioneer breeders as Elmer Claar, Carl Betscher, A. B. Stout, Elizabeth Nesmith, Ralph Wheeler, Hans Sass, and David Hall. Mary Lester was herself a pioneer in the field of *Hemerocallis* breeding:

> Years later, Dr. Kraus and I compared notes on the ones we began with, and the list was almost identical. The one exception was that he used GYPSY which I was afraid of because of its deep fulvous coloring which I disliked. He was wiser than I, but I saved myself a lot of work. This was to set the pattern for all breeding from then on—to follow the line of least resistance. Each color line was kept separate.

In 1960 she won the Stout Medal for her FAIRY WINGS. This was from her yellow line. FAIRY WINGS produced ruffles and green throats.

She considered Dr. Kraus's MULTNOMAH the greatest breakthrough in getting large melons.

Her other line was her "blue" line which came from DOROTHEA (Lester-Milliken) which was the first to have purple in the eyezone. She admitted that the coloring was not stable and was more accurately called violet.

Elizabeth Nesmith · 1953

If Mary Lester was the South's gracious lady pioneer among early Hemerocallis breeders, surely Elizabeth Nesmith was the *grande dame* of the North. Long before the formation of the American Hemerocallis Society, Elizabeth Nesmith had established herself as a highly respected hybridizer and grower of iris and daylilies. With this head start, she became a dominant force in the new Society. In 1950 she had 21 of her introductions on the Popularity Poll—more than any other hybridizer. (Dr. Stout was second.)

She was a personality to reckon with. Charter Member Howard Andros recalls:

> I daresay that most people seeing Elizabeth Nesmith in action for the first time in the late forties, were aware that they were in the presence of an extraordinary person. Although they would at once feel her gracious manner, they would also sense the qualities of a leader, even a capacity to manipulate people as readily as the creations in her garden.
>
> That she was the matriarch and forger of new styles, directions and standards for hybridizing *Hemerocallis* and iris in Eastern America, there was little room for doubt.

To visitors, she was gracious but reserved. It was not easy for strangers to plumb her sensitive mind. Many would never do so. However, there were cracks in the wall if one would but look. One was her garden. . . .

Recalling her aristocratic bearing and her impressive hats worn to ward off the sun, Massachusetts member Ruth Merry put it more simply. "At that time she was Mrs. Nesmith to everyone and it was years before we dared to call her Betty."

She was meticulous in record keeping as in other pursuits and recommended line breeding for at least three generations. Throughout her long career she worked with several color lines. As early as 1932, Mrs. Nesmith was fortunate to obtain one of the plants of *H. fulva* var. 'Rosea' from the collection sent by Dr. Arthur Steward to Dr. Stout. From this she evolved her pink line. Her own PINK PRELUDE was used extensively in the parentage of later introductions.

In 1952, Mrs. Nesmith was awarded the Stout Silver Medal for her red-purple POTENTATE.

Elizabeth Nesmith left several written records in the form of articles done for the *Hemerocallis*

photo courtesy Sydney Eddison

5.7. Elizabeth Nesmith, in one of her impressive hats worn to ward off the sun.

Journal, including an article that appeared in the first Yearbook. Her adherence to the Wilson Color Chart lent validity to her observations. She was a master at descriptive writing, never so evident as in her famous Fairmount Garden catalog.

Ezra J. Kraus - 1954

Another of the Society's notable early hybridizers was E.J. Kraus, a renowned plant scientist who over his long and distinguished teaching career held posts at several universities, including Oregon State, Michigan State, and the University of Chicago. It was during his 21-year tenure at the University of Chicago that he began his collection of over 1700 named daylilies. It was extraordinary for its time and provided a mecca for area growers and hybridizers. The garden and the man himself undoubtedly were factors in the collective productivity of that area.

Dr. Kraus was a born teacher. He fell naturally into the role of godfather to interested young scientists and aspiring plant breeders. "Interested" was the key word. He could be tolerant of human mistakes, but anything less than strict academic and personal integrity was not acceptable. This willingness to impart information carried over into his relationships outside the classroom.

During the ten years before his retirement from the University of Chicago, he began his intensive work with breeding chrysanthemums and daylilies. It was hoped that the field work would serve as a form of physical therapy following serious surgery. However, when in 1949 he prepared for his terminal leave from the University of Chicago, his health remained precarious. It was an adjustment for the former 210-pound, robust, mountain-climbing professor, but one he made with characteristic strength of will and determination.

Dr. Kraus's last move was to Corvallis, Oregon. In retirement there, he taught a laboratory class at Oregon State. Defying ill health, he continued his passion for plant breeding by having a chair brought into the field for his use while he made selections. During these final years he also engaged in a cooperative program with Edgar Lehman in Faribault, Minnesota, for testing in the Midwest. This required a difficult but not-to-be-missed annual pilgrimage to select daylily seedlings on site.

5-8. *Ezra J. Kraus, inspirational teacher.*

Although Dr. Kraus had a keen eye for color, other factors were of equal importance. He wanted strong, well-branched scapes, substance, and good foliage. He also watched for self-cleaning daylilies, daylilies that would shed their spent blooms cleanly within 48 hours. To this end he kept careful records, not just of the crosses themselves but of the results as well. He left 15 notebooks packed with field observations.

In 1963 he was awarded the Stout Medal for MULTNOMAH. Modest to a fault, it was not his nature to promote himself or his daylilies. It was left to Mr. Lehman to set a $50 price on MULTNOMAH, much to the dismay of Dr. Kraus who declared that no daylily was worth that much. He jokingly accused Mr. Lehman of selecting PINK LACE as a name for a daylily which, according to Dr. Kraus, was not pink and had no lace.

Another popular introduction and good parent was EVELYN CLAAR. This daylily remained at the top of the Popularity Poll for three consecutive years.

Many honors came to Dr. Kraus over the years, in the fields of both science and hybridizing. He often said that it was not his knowledge of plants that brought success, but his determination to see a thing through, regardless of the obstacles put in his path. It will come as no surprise that Dr. Kraus was a practitioner of that most patience-testing pursuit: line breeding.

OPHELIA TAYLOR - 1955

Surely detractors would cry "beginner's luck" to the unlikely event of a Stout Medal for a first introduction. Yet that was the case for Ophelia Taylor with her PRIMA DONNA in 1955. It was the first of the so-called polychrome daylilies and thus a stunning breakthrough. Three generations removed from her first cross between the species *H. aurantiaca* 'Major' and *H. fulva* var. 'Rosea,' it seemed an unlikely outcome. The first is orange gold while the second is a fulvous rose.

Although this winning cross was made in 1940, Ophelia Taylor's interest in daylilies was aroused in 1927 when she observed that several species in her Florida garden proved to be remarkably easy to grow. She began to collect in earnest. She tested all of Dr. Stout's introductions except CHARMAINE. Even as her collection grew, she was more interested during that period in identifying plants suited to Florida conditions than in hybridizing. Nevertheless, she picked up a second Stout Medal for her SALMON SHEEN in 1959.

In her early years, Ophelia Taylor did not concern herself with record keeping. Bill Munson recalls her shelling seeds as one would black-eyed peas and mixing them all in a bowl! After many friendly arguments he finally convinced her of the desirability of recording parentage. Some of her most serious hybridizing was done during the last five years of her life.

One goal—that of obtaining a super-fine pink—was never attained. It was to be a vigorous daylily with much dormancy in its background. She did achieve in one of her last hybrids, CHATEAUGAY, the vigor, beauty, and good garden habits she was seeking. Alas, the flower, though beautiful, was orange.

photo by Betty Hudson

5-9. *Ophelia (Mrs. Bright) Taylor, discussing the merits of an exhibit with Wilbur Harling. Mr. Harling was also a hybridizer from the Gainesville area.*

5-10. *David Hall, photographed among his iris, which were another great interest.*

David Hall · 1956

When AHS former President Paul Watts was living in the Chicago area, he found himself in the midst of a large group of prominent hybridizers. Dr. Kraus was certainly a leader. Then there was David Hall. Mr. Watts provides a bit of biography:

David Hall spent most of his working life as an attorney for the American Telephone and Telegraph company. Born in Canada, he came to Wilmette shortly after his marriage and almost immediately began growing flowers on his city-sized lot. Later he acquired a vacant property directly behind Orville Fay's earlier home and expanded his hybridizing activities. They were good personal friends with mutual interests in iris and eventually daylilies. Each benefited from the other's knowledge and experience.

Dave was responsible for bringing pink into the iris family and eventually created the earliest pink-tinted daylilies, working with *H. fulva* 'Rosea' and his own MISSION BELLS, an early star in the daylily world. He eventually earned the Bertrand Farr medal for hybridizing. By the time of the 1952 convention in Chicago, Dave's red daylilies—most of which had Dr. Kraus's things in their background—were widely admired and a highlight of the meeting. As his pink line improved, he finally produced the *Hemerocallis* he felt worthy of the name MAY HALL—an opinion confirmed by its earning the Stout Medal. Dr. Kraus had previously named one of his own daylilies MRS. DAVID HALL in her honor. Dave was an ardent advocate of line breeding, as opposed to Orville's program of utilizing occasional outcrosses to outstanding products of other hybridizers.

Dave became associated with Gilbert H. Wild & Son Nursery, and after about 1953 the Wilds handled all of his introductions. They were active in multiplying his seedlings as well as selecting ones for eventual introduction. The Wilds later established the David Hall Memorial Award to honor him.

We visited the Hall garden annually and never found him dressed casually; he was always wearing a shirt, tie, and hat, irrespective of the weather. At age 89 he bought a new car because "I just renewed my driver's license so I can drive for another three years." He did, too, eventually being killed by a train at 93 while walking in his suburban town.

Dave had interesting stories to tell of his many years experience—including the time Alexander Graham Bell visited his office in 1901. It was so warm on the evening of his 90th birthday party that Brother Charles commented that we were getting a foretaste of purgatory. Dave was very fond of a local restaurant called the Indian Trail. Going there with him occasionally, it was interesting to see him order apple pie and top it off with cream, sugar, and a blob of butter.

Ralph W. Wheeler · 1957

Ralph Wheeler was born in New York state, educated in the arts, and migrated to Florida in his middle years. That move kindled his first real awareness of the horticultural world.

Florida's exotic plant life impressed him so greatly that he began a collection of tropical plants. One of these was the *Amaryllis*. He became friends with well-known naturalists and horticulturists of the area. In 1933, he and three others organized the American Amaryllis Society (soon to become known as the American Plant Life Society). This organization was a pioneer in the study of *Hemerocallis*.

5-11. *Ralph W. Wheeler, one of four founders of the American Plant Life Society.*

5-12. *Hugh M. Russell, displaying the 1958 President's Cup winner, MARSHA RUSSELL.*

Mr. Wheeler took a scholarly interest in color. He noted that daylily flowers other than yellow were like velvet, made up of a backing and a pile and that these two parts were of different colors. He observed that when the sun strikes a red pile, it flattens and the backing becomes visible. Develop a red with a red backing, he reasoned, and the problem would be eliminated. This he did and RUBY SUPREME was born.

His frustration with verbal flower descriptions led him to assemble large slide collections which he made available on loan to interested parties all around the country.

Mr. Wheeler acquired two Stout Medals, for NARANJA in 1956 and PLAYBOY in 1961. He also received the President's Cup in 1960 for PLAYBOY.

Ralph Wheeler spent the remainder of his 82 years in his adopted home of Florida.

H. M. RUSSELL · 1958

H. M. (Hugh) Russell was the first broadly commercial grower of daylilies. Like the Gilbert Wild Nursery to follow, he distributed specialty daylilies to the general gardener and was the source of many daylily hobbyists' first purchases.

Born in Indian Territory—now Oklahoma—he experienced hunger and deprivation as a child. These hardships fed his determination to provide a better life for his own family. AHS Charter Member D. R. McKeithan was one of those who acquired his first collection from Russell:

Hugh Russell at that time (1941) not only advertised his daylilies in newspapers and flower magazines, but he would load up his truck and travel far and wide huckstering his daylilies to anyone who showed any interest in his truck full of flowers. He always did his hucksterring while the flowers were in bloom. He was a master merchandiser and would have succeeded in any venture he attempted.

His chosen venture led him to Spring, Texas, where he became the owner of the single largest planting of daylilies in the world.

Hugh Russell, hybridizer, did not give away too many of his trade secrets. His first crosses were *H. flava* and the difficult *H. fulva*. He later worked toward improved pinks with wider petals. It was his opinion that these would not come from *H. fulva* var. 'Rosea' which he considered to be a perpetrator of narrow petals.

AHS's second Stout Medal was awarded to Hugh Russell for his PAINTED LADY, still available commercially. He won the President's Cup in 1958 for MARSHA RUSSELL.

ELMER CLAAR - 1959

Again we turn to our roving reporter Paul Watts for recollections of one of the influential Chicago-area hybridizers:

> Elmer Claar—a teacher, lawyer, and real estate manager/developer—maintained the next largest collection of named daylilies in the Chicago area, after that of Dr. Kraus. Elmer grew his *Hemerocallis* in beds planted by color—contending this was the best way to make comparisons of cultivars, monitor improvements, appraise seedlings, and ensure against duplication. Actually, it was a great help to visiting judges in their work as well as to other daylily gardeners trying to reach decisions on purchases. He was fortunate in having a gardener to assist with much of the manual effort required to maintain his hobby and the extensive grounds of his property.
>
> Dr. Kraus named a breakthrough pink EVELYN CLAAR for Elmer's wife. Red was a particular interest of Elmer's and his BESS ROSS won the Stout Medal in 1954. He was awarded the Bertrand Farr and Helen Field Fischer Medals and served the Society as president. His hybrids were introduced by Parry Nurseries until his death. He donated the President's Cup to the Society and it has been a part of every convention up to the present.
>
> In addition to collecting and hybridizing daylilies, Elmer was a tireless collector of antique silver and snuff bottles. He was strongly committed to diploid culture until his death in the early 1960s and never introduced any tetraploids.

LeMOINE J. BECHTOLD - 1960

LeMoine Bechtold is the pride of Denver-area *Hemerocallis* growers. The 1960 winner of the Bertrand Farr Medal is best known for KINDLY LIGHT, the incomparable yellow spider that is still

5-13.
*Elmer Claar,
Chicago
hybridizer.*

used extensively as a parent and as a garden plant in its own right.

The Bechtold garden was a five-acre tract, nine miles south of Denver. A small stream running through the corner of the property permitted irrigation in this climate of low rainfall.

LeMoine was named by his mother for Victor LeMoine, the Luther Burbank of France. The strategy apparently worked. At an early age he developed a lifelong interest in flowers and shrubs. While carrying on his father's music business, he devoted his spare time to garden work and experiments.

5-14.
*LeMoine Bechtold,
named for a
French plantsman.*

5-15. Orville Fay, left, and David Hall—two Chicago area breeders. Orville Fay was a major player in the new tetraploid movement while David Hall sought clear pink in the diploids.

Noting in the daylily what he considered to be a virtue of daily self-renewal, he began to develop this plant. In 1922 he ordered every plant in the Gilbert H. Wild & Son catalog. At that time the variety was limited and included several of the species. After making use of these in various crosses, he contacted Allen Wild about marketing the LeMoine daylilies and thus a long-term relationship was struck.

From a twisting-petaled seedling that was to be named HAREM GIRL, he developed a strain of spider-like daylilies. LYDIA BECHTOLD and BLYTHE LADY, occasionally seen today, were recognized as heavy bloomers. SHIRLEY WILD was the largest and KINDLY LIGHT the most popular. While the form of the latter seems to vary from place to place, it is well liked wherever it is grown.

The Bechtold daylilies have enjoyed a revival with the renewed interest in spiders. A clump of the lemon yellow GARDEN PORTRAIT, registered in 1950, turned heads at a recent convention; and KINDLY LIGHT has never gone out of style.

HOOPER CONNELL · 1961

Hooper Connell lived, worked, and "played" at his hobby in the state of Louisiana. By profession, he was an engineer, educated at Cornell University in New York.

He began hybridizing daylilies in 1930, using hybrids from *H. citrina*, some seed from California, and whatever cultivars were available to him at the time. He sought daylilies that would be adaptable to the lower South. The peak of his success occurred in the late 1950s and early 1960s when he received several Awards of Merit.

In his first years of hybridizing he worked with reds. MARSE CONNELL, a red daylily introduced in 1952 and named for his grandfather, was widely grown. The following year he registered HEARTS AFIRE, which later took an Award of Merit.

A 1956 registration called MENTONE was described in the *Check List* as "pale old rose." This author has not seen it, but it received high praise in the 1962 *Yearbook* and two years later was honored with an Award of Merit.

In 1958 GAY LARK, a light red-orange polychrome won an Award of Merit.

Mr. Connell also worked with the pale yellow and near-white classes. SILVER SAILS earned him yet another Award of Merit as did DELTA GIRL, a light yellow.

Although he hybridized for many years, it was strictly a pursuit of pleasure. He kept no records because he did not want to make work of his hobby. It was only through the urging of his friends that he registered his hybrids. Hooper Connell was never ambitious for recognition and thus little information about his work exists in the Society literature.

Orville W. Fay - 1962

Like Dr. Stout before him, Orville Fay was a Wisconsin farm boy turned scientist. Following his study of cytology and genetics at River Falls State Teachers College, he married and moved to Wilmette, Illinois, where he took up his work as a plant breeder. He was involved with iris, chrysanthemums, and daylilies—in that order. As Steve Moldovan wrote, "For the next fifteen years he regarded the *Hemerocallis* as weeds with a great future if he could only get them out of the rut and into an active state of evolution."

In studying the published statements of this important pioneer in the tetraploid field, one can't escape the impression that this man was possessed of a healthy ego and strong opinions. Working in the Chicago area during its hybridizer heyday, he cites Dr. Kraus as the only pioneer breeder from whom he received help and inspiration. Nevertheless, the record shows that he worked at colchicine treatment of seeds with Dr. Robert Griesbach for several years before coming up with CRESTWOOD ANN. Mr. Fay states flatly, "CRESTWOOD ANN is the most important introduced tetraploid in the world today."

Besides giving respect due to Dr. Kraus as a fellow scientist, Orville Fay commended him for his generosity in the gift of EVELYN CLAAR. Now this was indeed of enormous help to Mr. Fay, for it became the starting point for all his work with pinks, roses, and melons. From it came FRANCES FAY which was unquestionably a milestone in his diploid breeding.

Once Mr. Fay began work with tetraploids, he made an emphatic case for their superiority.

He considered the theory of regional performance to be outdated and cited his FRANCES FAY as proof to the contrary. Indeed, he had success in crossing evergreen with deciduous plants to produce daylilies that bloomed well from Chicago to Houston. One gathered that they dared not do otherwise, having been genetically programmed, for Mr. Fay was very strong on Mendel's Law. He cautioned young hybridizers to make the second generation cross before becoming discouraged, for it was in that cross that the desirable recessive traits would exhibit themselves.

The "Crestwood" series was an important base for the future of tetraploids as was Mr. Fay's decision make tetraploid parents more accessible to other breeders by reducing the price of his own stock.

Orville Fay was to receive four Stout Medals—for FRANCES FAY, CARTWHEELS, SATIN GLASS, and MARY TODD. Surely, his was a remarkable career that earned him the right to his opinions.

Frank Childs - 1963

Although Frank Childs of Georgia never won the Stout Medal, this gentle man contributed an impressive number of advances in the field of hybridizing and produced a host of daylilies that were sought after by gardeners everywhere. His 1951 PINK

5-16. *Frank Childs (photo 1964), excelled in delicate colors.*

DREAM was a first in the good clear pink class that hybridizers had long been seeking. This was followed by PEGGY CHILDS, named for his wife, who worked at his side throughout their years together.

Perhaps his most important introduction was CATHERINE WOODBERY. The pale orchid with its chartreuse throat captivated growers and breeders alike. The color was unusual for its day. It was one of the most heavily used diploid parents in the 1960s and beyond. Although many of his daylilies had hints of blue, the true blue daylily was to elude him as it has others.

The goal of white was advanced with the introduction of ICE CARNIVAL. This was followed by the popular SERENE MADONNA and other near-whites.

When tetraploids came on the scene, Frank Childs started a line from his own conversions. CATHERINE WOODBERY, a natural choice, proved difficult, but he succeeded in getting a chimeral fan from a treated plant. With successful conversion, CATHERINE WOODBERY added a new dimension to the work of leading tetraploid breeders such as Munson and Peck.

Most of Frank Childs's work centered on delicate colors, but he did experiment with a red tetraploid line. Unfortunately, the bright reds tended to melt in the heat of Piedmont, Georgia.

All of Frank Childs's crosses were meticulously recorded in a stud book.

5-17. *Hamilton P. Traub, scientist and American Plant Life Society editor* of HERBERTIA.

HAMILTON P. TRAUB · 1964

Dr. Traub was by profession a physiologist and geneticist. His roots were in the Midwest, but his serious work with daylilies began in 1932 in central Florida as an offshoot of his lifelong interest in the *Amaryllidaceae* family, which includes *Hemerocallis*.

Several references in this anniversary publication give credit to the American Plant Life Society as an unofficial cornerstone in the formation of AHS. Dr. Traub was one of the organizers of the APLS, along with Ralph Wheeler and Wyndham Hayward. Further, Dr. Traub was editor of that society's scholarly publication, *Herbertia*. The APLS assisted the fledgling Hemerocallis Society by releasing substantive articles for reprint in the early *Yearbooks*. In fact, one of Dr. Traub's own papers was published in the first *Yearbook* edited by Gretchen Harshbarger.

In the 1940s Dr. Traub moved to Maryland and began a program of tetraploid breeding for the United States Department of Agriculture at Beltsville. He introduced a series: TETRA STARZYNSKI, TETRA APRICOT, TETRA PEACH, and others which were distributed free to the public by the USDA.

In 1952 he retired and moved to La Jolla, California, and, to a busier life than ever. There he continued with his editing of *Herbertia*, scientific writing, and plant classification. Also, he continued to breed tetraploid *Hemerocallis*. During this period he introduced three series which he arranged to benefit the American Plant Life Society. The series, rather unimaginatively called "The First California Series," "The Second California Series," and "The Third California Series," were each made up of plants dominated by given characteristics. Most were evergreen. The third series was built on the first and second plus additional converted diploids. By special arrangement, Julia Hardy of Alabama introduced several cultivars from the California Series.

Dr. Traub's introductions include GOLDEN GLOW (1938), SAFFRON BEAUTY (1959), LUCRETIUS (1959), and CORAL MASTERPIECE (1965). VELVET BUTTERFLY was considered by some discerning growers to be his best; a 1967 price list from Iron Gate Gardens shows VELVET BUTTERFLY going for $50.00—big bucks for a daylily thirty years ago.

Edna Spalding - 1965

From two plant purchases, ROSALIND and KILLARNEY LASS, Edna Spalding made her first crosses in 1940. Twelve to fifteen generations later she produced her first pink, FRONTIER LADY. From that moment forward, Miss Edna, as she was affectionately known, became a Louisiana success story.

Her early years were marked by hard work, illness, and the death of her parents. She helped neighbors harvest rice and babies, and worked on a truck farm.

After her initial success with FRONTIER LADY, Miss Edna occasionally outcrossed to selected stock, but most of her crosses were planned from her "Hem Patch" where she exercised a discriminating eye for characteristics that might further her goals. It was her practice to select what she considered the most outstanding bloom of the day and to use its pollen for all her crosses that day.

As her plants attracted nationwide attention, many visitors found their way to her garden in Iowa, Louisiana. She credited Dr. Corliss for giving her a boost with a big write-up in *Horticulture* magazine.

One very popular introduction was DORCAS. Her own favorites, she said, were "ANGEL CHOIR and JUBILEE PINK for length of bloom, and LAVENDER FLIGHT for sheer beauty and depth of color." The most awards went to LUXURY LACE. This small flower received the Stout Medal, a David Hall Medal, and the Annie T. Giles Award.

Not the least of Miss Edna's contributions was the legacy left to her niece Elsie Spalding who took delivery on five talents and, like the good servant, returned five more.

W. B. MacMillan - 1966

W. B. MacMillan was one of the most influential hybridizers to practice in a territory replete with horticultural giants. His long years of work with Louisiana iris and daylilies began with his move to Abbeville, Louisiana. He was himself influenced by breeders in the area, most notably Edna Spalding.

"Mr. Mac" was born in Texas in 1883. Not unlike others of this vintage and locale, he began his primary education in a one-room schoolhouse. After completing his secondary training at Southwestern

5-18. *Edna Spalding, a Louisiana success story.*

University in Georgetown, he married and moved to New Jersey where he continued his studies and became a principal of public schools.

An abrupt change in careers took him to Louisiana. He left the field of education and became involved in the rice industry. This new business was to claim his vocational years until retirement at the age of eighty.

His lifelong avocation was horticulture. He moved from Louisiana iris to camellias to daylilies. Being an opportunist by nature, he finally settled on daylilies because he saw in them more potential for improvement and profit.

The W. B. MacMillan name has become synonymous with the popular flat, round daylily, but he did not invent the form. He expanded on the work of Edna Spalding, a friend and noted hybridizer of the day. Stock purchased from her garden was carefully selected to advance the breeding of pinks and lavenders. Unlike Miss Edna, Mr. Mac soon gave up on tetraploids.

"Peggy Mac" was very involved with her husband's hobby. She kept an accurate stud book of all his crosses. After a household accident in 1969, she became an invalid and Lucille Guidry was employed as her nurse. When Mrs. MacMillan died, Mrs. Guidry remained as full-time nurse for the aging Mr. Mac. It was through his nurturing of her interest in daylilies that the AHS gained one of its most skillful hybridizers. Likewise, Mr. Mac's gardener, Olivier Monette, took lessons from the master and became well-known in the hybridizing field.

The first of Mr. Mac's Stout Medals was awarded for CLARENCE SIMON, a melon-colored daylily with excellent plant habits and wide petals for the time. Using this as a parent, he anticipated great things, but his hopes were dashed once the seedlings bloomed. None of the prodigy surpassed the parent.

In 1979, he won his second Stout Medal for MOMENT OF TRUTH, a popular near-white daylily. Then came SABIE, the 1983 winner, a large, low-growing bright yellow with wide, creped petals.

Perhaps Mr. Mac's biggest disappointment was with his EDNA SPALDING MEMORIAL, a beautiful greenish yellow named in honor of the hybridizer to whom he owed his start. Alas, the plant was genetically flawed, subject to a mysterious "sudden death syndrome."

Most of Mr. MacMillan's work was with pinks, lavenders, and near whites. However, he did introduce JUMBO RED, a very full rose red that was used successfully as a parent in spite of some eccentric foliage habits.

Another of his daylilies, AGGIE SELLERS, was used by hybridizers, including Lucille Guidry, for its beautiful form and coloring. This gave rise to her own Stout Medal winner, JANET GAYLE.

The MacMillan hybrids were ahead of their time in flower form and consequently fit comfortably alongside more recent full-blown garden beauties.

R. W. MUNSON, JR. - 1967

The story of Bill Munson's hybridizing is a continuing saga, best told by Mr. Munson himself. This he has done in the handsomely illustrated edition of *Hemerocallis: The Daylily.* Professionally trained as an architect, he maintained his intense avocation in parallel with his career. He introduced his first daylily at the age of 25.

His family's involvement is complex. His mother Ida, who died in 1994, has several registrations in her name. Sister Betty Hudson and niece Elizabeth Hudson Salter also hybridize. Much of this productivity had its start on the large grounds of Wimberlyway Gardens in Gainesville, Florida, where the family located in 1968.

Bill Munson's breeding program has favored pastels. Important in his first group of cream and ivory through lavender-orchid was SPRING WALTZ, derived from Show Girl X (Mission Bells

5-19.
*W. B. MacMillan,
famous for round,
ruffled daylily form.
The lady on the left is
Mr. Mac's wife, Peggy.
(1966)*

photo by Bertha Cone

x Prima Donna). In a 1962 *Hemerocallis Journal*, he describes an amusing charge by Peter Fass that was made at the national convention:

> Peter cornered me first by a question that went something like this, "I used MISSION BELLS and got no seedlings from it I could keep. I used PRIMA DONNA and nothing from it. And I used SHOW GIRL and got nothing of any consequence. Now Munson, tell me how you could have gotten anything by combining all three?" Well, what can you say to such a tightly knit argument? But it does prove one point as I see it. It is not necessarily one parent, but the combination of two parents that can or does give the desired effect.

The second important line was melon-cream through pink. These were just the beginning. Much water has passed under the bridge since then, and Bill Munson has even established an impressive line of reds, based on Munson, Peck, and Moldovan cultivars, and on induced SAIL ON (Claar).

Orville Fay's contention that crossing evergreen with dormant would eliminate the problem of regional daylilies proved to be an oversimplification. However, Mr. Munson tried much the same thing and did succeed in producing a hardier line of evergreens than had come out of the area heretofore. Many of the Munson daylilies performed very well in the North.

When the tetraploid frenzy began, Bill Munson got with the program. It was a difficult period in that the early tetraploids appeared to be a step backward. Now, a majority of his line are tet. His parentages, reflected in his seedling numbers, are complicated.

A unique contribution from Mr. Munson's program was the evolution of a new color pattern that was to be termed a "watermark"—a chalky blotch surrounding the throat.

He has further developed the fringed gold edge. There are now improvements on Ida Munson's famous IDA'S MAGIC. Dark edgings too, combined with a matching eye such as in PANACHE were exciting breakthroughs.

Outstanding developments over the years are too numerous to catalog here, but they include such examples as KINGS CLOAK, MAGNIFIQUE (important as a parent), CHATEAU BLANC (basis of

5-20. *R. W. Munson, Jr., early in his career.*

photo courtesy Munson

the near-white program), WATER BIRD (for color patterns), HIGH LAMA (for more rounded form in the blue-purple coloring), OLIVE BAILEY LANGDON, RUSSIAN RHAPSODY, SARI, HIGHLAND LORD, BENCHMARK, KATE CARPENTER, FRED HAM, ELIZABETH ANN HUDSON and PANACHE. Many of these played significant roles as parents and are to be found in the lines of other hybridizers.

Despite his primary avocation of daylily breeding, Bill Munson found time to share his knowledge with others and to serve a term as AHS president.

Hubert Fischer - 1968

Worthy as it is, Hubert Fischer's hybridizing is almost eclipsed by his monumental service to the Society, for which he received the Helen Field Fischer Medal. It should not be forgotten, however, that he was also one of the Chicago Area Hybridizers—by now a group that has earned capital status by its frequent appearance on this list of Bertrand Farr winners.

Mr. Fischer was always interested in the miniatures. Through his friendship with Dr. Kraus he obtained pollen from seedlings of two small flowers

5-21. *Hubert Fischer. Great daylilies in small packages.*

plus the warning that no one would be interested in this size. Undaunted, Mr. Fischer persisted with the line that eventually produced his first miniature, TINY TOT, in 1949. In another three years he had GOLDEN CHIMES and THUMBELINA, both of which were major attractions at the 1953 Chicago Convention and went on to receive many awards. Later he added another winner, CORKY, thoroughly disproving his friend Dr. Kraus's pessimistic prediction. To encourage more interest in the minis and to honor the memory of their only son, the Fischers

5-22. *Wilmer B. Flory, tireless worker for the Society.*

donated the sterling trophy, the Donn Fischer Memorial Cup. Hubert was voted the award himself on three occasions for the popular triad above.

From Ophelia Taylor's PRIMA DONNA and Dr. Kraus's RUTH LEHMAN, he created CONTESSA. Thus began a line outside the miniature class.

Many of Hubert Fischer's daylilies had remarkable staying power. They were good garden plants and can be found in landscapes today. The deep red ORIENTAL RUBY is a sunfast red with bud-building habit. BURNING DAYLIGHT is still one of the most intense orange-gold selfs around and positively glows across the garden, pointy petals notwithstanding. And, of course, we come face to face with his GREEN VALLEY every time we look at the AHS logo.

WILMER B. FLORY · 1969

Wilmer Flory of Logansport, Indiana, was another Charter Member who gave a great deal of himself to the Society. His long-term service as editor left us with a series of meaty, thoughtfully edited *Journals* that make very interesting reading today. He was a teacher by profession, congenial by nature, and a wonderful communicator. He was a popular banquet speaker with an endless supply of appropriate stories. At one convention, Judge Cary Quinn introduced him as the "Will Rogers of Indiana."

As a breeder of iris, he fell naturally into hybridizing daylilies once he began collecting. He also had a fine collection of daffodils.

Mr. Flory bought his first daylilies in 1919 from Bertrand Farr for $3.00 each. This was quite a bit, he explained, when he was getting $35 a month teaching.

His crowning achievement was AVA MICHELLE, winner of the 1970 Stout Medal. This, he pointed out, is a bud builder. It is sterile. FRITZ ROHWEDER is a fragrant gold and is still available. Another popular Flory origination was FRANS HALS, a late-blooming bicolor. FLYING SAUCER, an Award of Merit winner, is a pale yellow of overwhelming dimensions.

The 1976 MED was cited as Mr. Flory's own favorite. It is a strong grower, a characteristic that the hybridizer espoused. "For heaven's sake, breed

5-23. *Robert A. Griesbach, scientist with special interest in seed germination. He has done extensive research on both daylilies and true lilies (Lilium).*

vigor into them right from the start—balance, quality, substance."

Who knows to what heights Wilmer Flory might have flown had he not been so busy helping his young Society to get on its feet.

ROBERT A. GRIESBACH - 1970

Robert Griesbach was born in Manasha, Wisconsin, but work on his Ph.D. brought him to Chicago where he became one of the famous Chicago-area hybridizers. His thesis, prepared at the University of Chicago under the late Paul Voth, was "Dormancy and Seed Germination in Hemerocallis." We turn again to Paul Watts for his remembrances of Dr. Griesbach:

> Dr. Robert Griesbach is the youngest of the hybridizers who attained prominence in the Chicago area. He developed an early interest in horticulture and eventually became a professor in the subject at De Paul University. He is a cytologist and geneticist and spent much time with Dr. Voth, who succeeded Dr. Kraus at the University of Chicago. His first hybridizing work was with gladiolus and his creations earned numerous awards and prizes. He eventually came to know Orville Fay and used some of Orville's excess acreage to grow his corms.

He then went into a joint effort with Orville in creating tetraploid daylilies. He had the technical ability and background for the project and with Orville's enthusiasm and available materials they created the "Crestwood" series via the colchicine route. Bob earned the Farr medal for hybridizing, concentrating his efforts on red daylilies where he has achieved some fine results. In the early years his creations were handled by Julia Hardy; now they are introduced by the Klehm organization. In addition to daylilies Bob has a strong interest in true lilies and grew them in quantity years ago when we visited his garden. [He converted and bred tetraploid true lilies.]

Dr. Griesbach has returned to his home state of Wisconsin in his retirement. There he continues to do research in seed germination, especially in true lilies, but also with daylilies. His son, also a plant geneticist, does research for the USDA at Beltsville, Maryland. Young Dr. Griesbach may be distinguished from his father by the middle initial *J*. He is an AHS member and occasional contributor to the *Daylily Journal*.

Robert A. Griesbach was a major player in the "tetraploid convention" of 1961. His older sunfast, garden-worthy red tetraploids such as ARRIBA and MARION BRODNAX are still grown and appreciated by many AHS members.

George E. Lenington - 1970

In 1945, George Lenington was tuned to radio station KFNF and heard Helen Field Fischer's invitation to convene in Shenandoah for the great daylily party. Thus he became Number 761 in the Midwest Hemerocallis Society. He was very active in the early days of the organization, serving a term in every office.

His introduction to gardening began in Kansas several years earlier. His parents ran a small nursery where his interest, he recalls, "was whetted by enforced periods of weed elimination." He later studied floriculture at the University of Kansas. In 1946 he became superintendent of building and grounds at the home office of Kansas City Life Insurance Company. It was there that his real work with daylilies began. A mutually satisfactory arrangement was made to beautify the grounds with Mr. Lenington's 260 *Hemerocallis* cultivars.

Later, George Lenington married and with his wife and partner Lucille began Lenington Nurseries in Kansas City. Both George and Lucille hybridized.

One special interest was to develop daylilies that would thrive all over the United States. To encourage breeding in this direction, he donated the Lenington All-American Award.

The first Lenington introduction was McPICK. (It was selected by D.R. McKeithan; the name derived from "Mac's Pick.") It captured the Annie T. Giles award. Then came LOLABELLE which won the President's Cup in 1968. Both of these small yellow flowers are still grown.

Some of his best daylilies came as a result of his goal to develop a pure white. LUCILLE LENINGTON, named for his first wife, was one of these. He considered CREAM MAGIC to be his whitest, but he preferred GOING PLACES for its 50 buds on a scape. Good branching and bud count was another goal. Probably his most well-known daylily is MAVIS SMITH, named for an equally well-known daylily connoisseur of Columbia, Missouri. Selected by Mavis herself, the flawless form and recessive pastel coloring have made it an effective parent for other colors.

Through his friendship with Jim Marsh of Chicago, Mr. Lenington acquired an interest and stock in the new tetraploids. All the "Mokan" series are tetraploid.

An accident along the way was RED RIBBONS. He never intended to do spiders, but visitors finally persuaded him to introduce this one and subsequently it won the Harris Olson Spider Award.

At the time of his death—he was then in his eighties—Mr. Lenington was pursuing a goal for a good clear pink. ZENA was named in honor of his friend and neighbor, Zena Purdum. The daylily is registered as Midseason, but would more accurately be placed in the rarefied Late classification.

photo courtesy Bob Lenington

5-24. *George Lenington, held all the offices of AHS.*

Sally Lake - 1971

Sally Lake's interest in daylilies began in Selma, Alabama, when she received a gift of daylily fans from a Charter Member of AHS. She was impressed by the performance of this versatile plant and was inspired to study all the literature on its cultivation. She purchased the latest hybrids from leading hybridizers. Dr. Kraus had the greatest influence on her hybridizing program.

In 1950 she moved her four-year collection to Mobile. The daylily was little known in that city, but she changed that. Here she produced SILVER KING which was honored by an Award of Merit.

All in all, she registered 22 daylilies for which she received 8 Honorable Mentions. Her last registration was WINNING BEAUTY. This was awarded the AHS Achievement Medal at the 1967 Mobile Hemerocallis Show.

The Sally Lake Memorial Award was established in her honor as an incentive to hybridizers in Region 14.

VIRGINIA PECK - 1972

Scientist, AHS officer and director, writer—all of these apply to Virginia Peck; but here we will be concerned with her hybridizing—no small subject in itself.

She attained her doctorate from Vanderbilt University and was a full professor of English at Middle Tennessee State University. However, she later studied cytology and genetics and became an expert in both. This remarkable woman usually succeeded in whatever she attempted, be it Olympic diving or horticulture.

Fast-forwarding through a nontraditional career and marriage to Richard Peck, we arrive at the Chicago "tetraploid convention" where Dr. Richard and Dr. Virginia find themselves among the great scientists of the *Hemerocallis* world. Life will never be the same again.

For all practical purposes, Virginia Peck's hybridizing career began with the tetraploids. With her inquiring mind, she probed the depths of existing information and then struck out on her own. The Peck home was expanded to include a well-equipped laboratory and an electric greenhouse.

She worked with several lines, but one of the most productive was her red line. SIR PATRICK SPENS was the first introduction from this line. Then came DOUGLAS DALE and LUSTY LELAND. There were others, but these three were important parents used by Virginia and many other hybridizers.

About the same time, she started a line out of BONNIE BARBARA ALLEN that was to yield several advances in pastel shades of pink or melon. QUEEN ELEANOR and HEATHER GREEN were breakthroughs in the line.

In 1971 she generated excitement with her clear yellow EVENING BELL. This was followed by the triangular, light yellow FLORENCE BYRD.

5-25.
*Virginia Peck,
"First Lady of
Tetraploids."*

In 1977 she won the Robert P. Miller award for the best near-white tetraploid with ASTOLAT. Ten years later the James E. Marsh Award came her way for VIOLET HOUR, judged the best purple or lavender cultivar that year.

Her long line of successes would have been impressive even without DANCE BALLERINA DANCE, but that one accomplishment changed the face of tetraploids today. From it came a host of "DBD" seedlings with a degree of ruffling that had never before been seen in the tets. Virginia Peck acknowledged that DBD was not a finished flower in that it often had problems unfurling all its ruffles. But it was an enormously important parent used by breeders everywhere.

One of the characteristics that marked Virginia Peck throughout her association with the American Hemerocallis Society was her willingness to share information. She contributed an impressive number of articles and scientific papers to the Society for publication in the *Journal*. These continue to be a valuable resource to other hybridizers today. Perhaps one day they will be bound.

The title First Lady of Tetraploids suits Virginia Peck well.

CHARLES RECKAMP - 1973

At this writing Brother Charles (as he is best known) has been hybridizing daylilies for more than forty years. Encouraged by the Chicago-area hybridizers in their heyday, he was to become an important

photo courtesy Reg 2 N.L.

5-26. *Brother Charles Reckamp, working with his daylilies.*

factor in the advancement of tetraploids. In 1987 Paul Watts wrote the following account:

Brother Charles Reckamp spent much of his life at the Monastery of the Society of the Divine Word— about a mile from Orville Fay's daylily plantings. He originated in Missouri and operated a large nursery for his society [monastery] for many years, becoming very knowledgeable about perennials, shrubs and trees. He has hybridized many notable iris, worked with daylilies for years and began introducing them before 1950. The other hybridizers living near his Mission Garden Nursery became friends and fellow hobbyists. We met Orville Fay during a visit to Brother Charles's planting before our marriage. He was an enthusiastic follower of Orville's concepts and his hybrids have a great deal of Fay material in their background.

Brother Charles became interested in tetraploids when the treating of seeds with colchicine first commenced and for many years has produced only tetraploids in his seedlings. Steve Moldovan introduced his creations for some years and at present Klehm Nurseries handles all of his output. He received the Bertrand Farr medal in recognition of his hybridizing results. After almost sixty years in his

religious order, he is still actively crossing and raising daylilies. He also maintains the floral and landscaping features of the monastery now that his former nursery has been discontinued. LITTLE RAINBOW was one of his best known diploids and DAWN BALLET[*] is probably the most widely distributed of his tetraploids. Any spare time he has is spent working with stained glass and "rocks."

As evolved from Orville Fay's "Crestwood" line, Brother Charles's daylilies have featured pastel blends and shades of melon. He does not like recurve, preferring all segments to be completely visible for front viewing. The apricot-colored COMMAND-MENT introduced in 1966 was his first significant achievement.

Brother Charles may have been the first to put gold fringe or lacing around tetraploids. At least this new trait became a trademark in such celestial introductions as HEAVENLY TREASURE, AN-GELS DELIGHT, and HEAVENLY CROWN.

---

[*]DAWN BALLET may have been overtaken by the more interesting edged creations noted above.

photo by Bertha Cone

5-27. *James Marsh (1969), Chicago hybridizer who did pioneer work in lavenders and purples.*

James E. Marsh - 1974

The last of the great Chicago-area breeders to win the Bertrand Farr Award was James Marsh, a transported Kansan. Paul Watts remembers him well:

Using a small city lot, supplemented by a portion of a neighbor's back yard, he first became known in Chicago horticultural circles for his award-winning dahlia creations. As time passed, he moved into iris and created some excellent and popular cultivars. During this time he became acquainted with Orville Fay and David Hall and gradually worked into daylilies as their popularity increased. Pollen and plants from these men were prominent in Jim's early results. His initial introductions bore the preface "Prairie" in their names and he was one of the very first to work toward and actually achieve lavender coloration in his flowers. Probably PRAIRIE BLUE EYES was the most popular of his diploids in this color range.

When tetraploids came to the fore, Jim began working with them also. Eventually, he began introducing the "Chicago" series through Lenington Nurseries in Kansas City. His first two lavender/purple creations, CHICAGO REGAL and CHICAGO ROYAL, formed the basis for most other hybridizers' work in the colors. Jim also grew fantastic clematis, and his wife, Searcy, added exceptionally fine annuals to the garden.

Jim was awarded the Bertrand Farr Medal for his hybridizing efforts, and after his death Searcy established the James E. Marsh Award for the lavender/purple daylily receiving the most votes from AHS judges each year. [The award ran for a designated period of 10 years.]

After Jim's death, Klehm Nurseries acquired most of his seedlings and stock of some of his introductions, and they currently market many of them.

Early in his hybridizing career James Marsh revealed that he liked "to work with all the available daylily colors as I do not wish our garden to be identified with any one color." Nevertheless, so successful was he with the purples and lavenders that they did become associated with his name. Perhaps he might have been pleased with the posthumous introduction, JAMES MARSH, a brilliant red without a trace of blue.

5-28. *Allen J. Wild, of a famous nursery in Sarcoxie, Missouri.*

Allen J. Wild - 1975

After Allen Wild was presented the Bertrand Farr Award in 1975, Mavis Smith told the story of his interesting family heritage:

Allen J. Wild grew up in a family very involved in plants. In 1885 his grandfather purchased $45.00 worth of peonies for his son, Gilbert, who was then 8 years old. When Gilbert was 11 he shipped a crate of cut peonies to Nebraska in a carload of strawberries. He received $3.00 for these and this venture encouraged him to continue to grow peonies. Little did he know then what he was starting and how this was to influence the life of his son and his family. The firm of Gilbert H. Wild & Son that was formed later became a family affair, and continued to grow and become the peony center of the world. After his father's death in 1938 Allen became the head of the business. Later when Gene and Jim graduated from the University of Missouri they joined their father and mother, Haidee, and "The Wilds of Missouri" continue to work very closely together. (1975)

Peonies made way for iris and daylilies, with daylilies becoming increasingly important to the business. Selecting seedlings was a family affair. The fields were so large that several eyes kept watch lest a future star be overlooked. Promising plants were

5-29.
*John R.
Lambert, Jr.,
exponent of
individuality.*

moved to a more favorable location for closer observation. Out of this sifting process came WINNING WAYS, the large, light yellow awarded the Stout Medal in 1974.

Two small flowers, MELON BALLS and BAMBI DOLL won the Annie T. Giles Award and WINNIE THE POOH was runner-up for the Donn Fischer Memorial Cup.

Other Wild favorites have been BRAVE WORLD, GERALDINE DEAN, and the fragrant CASHMERE which won an Award of Merit. POST TIME was a very ruffled and very expensive red. In the same period another popular red, WALLY

5-30.
*Clara Mae
Pittard,
influenced by
W.B.
MacMillan.*

NANCE, was introduced. Two very large creped pastel blends, BEN ARTHUR DAVIS and ARCHANGEL, received wide distribution.

Some time after Allen Wild's death, his adult children, Gene and Jim, relinquished control of the nursery although it still bears the family name.

JOHN R. LAMBERT, JR. - 1976

John Lambert of Raleigh, North Carolina, was an individualist—a master of language, whose biting wit can be found in the pages of several back issues of the *Journal*.

The larger part of his hybridizing career was spent working exclusively with diploids. He did not immediately embrace the tetraploid movement, stating that he was too old to start over. Later, however, when he was older yet and in poor health, friends suggested tetraploid breeding as a tonic for the doldrums. He then embarked upon a program based on three of his own converted diploids and Virginia Peck's DANCE BALLERINA DANCE). In a further departure from an early stance, he chose to distinguish his tetraploid series by the prefix "Hermitage."

Dr. Lambert never followed the trends in hybridizing. As his friend Robert Savage said of his work, "The distinctiveness of Lambert daylilies is their very lack of a breeder's hallmark." Of his program, Dr. Lambert said, "I breed for breaks." It was not for him, the oft-stated recommendation to select a specific goal and stick to it with dogged determination. This was the road to boredom. His cultivars are as complex and eccentric as the man himself. In following his own path he produced an exceptionally broad range of colors, forms, and patterns.

His mixed gene pool has extended the daylily bloom season from spring until late fall. He was also a pioneer in nocturnal extenders.

Fragrance, too, found its way into Lambert cultivars. The first L. Plouf Constantly Very Fragrant Award went to WILLARD GARDNER.

CLARA MAE PITTARD - 1977

As a resident of Louisiana, Clara Mae Pittard was influenced by the hybridizing of W. B. MacMillan. She chose his GODDESS and AZREAL to begin her work. AZREAL was in the background of her line of large light yellows such as AMERICAN DREAM and IRISH SPRING.

She also hybridized small flowers, especially reds. A pair of these—GIDGET, very bright, and BRIDGET, very dark—were popular garden subjects.

In 1978 her small-flowered, RED RUM, a brick red shade, made an outstanding show in the Pittsburgh convention tour gardens, whereupon it was voted the Florida Sunshine Cup.

LUCILLE WILLIAMSON - 1978

Relatively few hybridizers have specialized in small flowers. Hubert Fischer was one of the first to buck the trend successfully. However, colors were still mostly limited to yellow and orange. It remained for Lucille Williamson of Texas to broaden the palette and improve form.

Her small-flowered, magnificently branched GREEN FLUTTER, still in the yellow class, is one of her most famous credits. With it she climbed the ladder of the award system to capture the Stout Medal. GREEN FLUTTER also won the Annie T. Giles Award.

Another milestone was LITTLE GRAPETTE. This miniature grape purple has been hard to surpass in its class. At the Shreveport convention in 1992, the aging charmer—registered in 1970—sailed past many newer entries to claim the Florida Sunshine Cup. It is also a Donn Fischer Award winner for best miniature. Lucille's "pink" line produced her second Donn Fischer Award in 1980 for LITTLE CELENA.

Lucille Williamson was probably the first to develop the eyed miniature and small flowers. Chief among these is LITTLE SHOWOFF which is still an outstanding garden plant.

Although she devoted most of her energies to her favored small flowers, Lucille produced some excellent daylilies that fall in the large-flowered class. One of these was MAMIE SCHULZE, a medium sized, frilly bloom in coral pink.

R. M. KENNEDY, III - 1979

Genial Bob Kennedy of South Carolina was another hybridizer who included miniatures in his repertoire. They were not his exclusive interest, but

5-31. Lucille Williamson, a touch of magic with miniature and small flowers.

they probably brought him the greatest attention. For a while he dominated the Donn Fischer Award list. To date, he is the only hybridizer in the history of AHS to win this award three consecutive years. The winners were all yellow: PUDDIN, BUTTER-PAT, and RAINDROP.

In the next-up size class he produced the 4-inch SUZIE WONG, another popular yellow which was to win the Annie T. Giles Award for best small flower in 1971. His second Giles Award was LORD CAMDEN, a ruffled, brilliant red.

Bob Kennedy's large flowers came in a multiplexity of hues. A primary goal was to produce pure, clear color; STRAWBERRY VELVET, an Award of Merit in 1979, typified his efforts. This is a clear strawberry-rose.

Before his death, Bob was doing serious work with late-blooming daylilies. The class had been neglected and the gene pool was limited. Most of the available Lates and Very Lates were light-years behind in color and form. Bob introduced CHROME PINK, registered as Late, and VOLUPTUOUS PINK as Mid-late—both improvements on existing Late daylilies. The newer ROYAL JESTER is a late-blooming, strawberries-and-cream bicolor. KIRKWOOD, another Late, is a small-flowered lavender and rose blend. Probably his best registered Late is WILLIE LYLES, a rose-pink and cream bitone, edged pink. Other colors were being selected, but his work in

photo by Harvey Horne

5-32. *Bob Kennedy, his serious intent always overlaid by a glorious smile.*

the area was destined to be passed into other hands. With the stimulus of the Eugene Foster Award, interest in better late-flowering daylilies has been sparked among other hybridizers.

ELSIE SPALDING · 1980

Following in the footsteps of her aunt, the famous Edna Spalding, Elsie Spalding made the road to Iowa, Louisiana, a well-traveled highway. Arguably, her daylilies were the most popular diploids from the late 1970s until her death in 1994.

She was not always so confident. Left with Miss Edna's stock and a few precious words of wisdom, Elsie Spalding wavered. "When Miss Edna left Bill and me her garden, I was so sure that I couldn't carry on as she had that my first thought was to sell many of the daylilies . . . that I couldn't do much more. Then I began to remember things she had told me as we worked together."

Plucking up her courage, she started in the spring of 1969. "Of course I knew what I liked—the soft pinks, yellows, lavenders, and blends. I realized that I did not like those that were not sunfast and melted in the hot sun. But above all I was afraid of ruining Miss Edna's line of flower successes."

The "Spalding pinks"—Elsie's—became a standard by which to measure excellence. Her diploids were used as a case against tetraploids. She had the form, the ruffling, and the color. Who needed tets?

Nobody knew quite how Elsie Spalding got her results. Some attributed it to a mystical instinct. That she did not keep records was used as a case against "science." None of these negative hypotheses were the instigation of Elsie herself. She had only a rudimentary education and did not often discuss such things. Yet, hopeful breeders and growers from all walks of life beat a path to her doorstep, hoping to talk Elsie out of the latest admired cultivar or seedling.

The list of exquisite Spalding introductions is too lengthy to consider in this space. Her work was with pinks and pastels and a few good clear yellows.

photo by Clarence Crochet

5-33. *Elsie Spalding. Her daylilies spoke for her.*

For years she had *the* "baby-ribbon pink" daylilies. These exquisite blooms shouted "quality," across the garden, across zone lines, and across the ocean.

She never sought awards. (It is an interesting comment on the awards system that one of her Stout Medal winners never received a Junior Citation.) Although her apolitical approach cost her some minor awards, she won in several major categories. In 1988 she received the Stout Medal for her MARTHA ADAMS. Her entry of LULLABY BABY in the small-flowered class won the Annie T. Giles Award in 1982. Two of her eyed daylilies were honored with the Don C. Stevens Award: WILL RETURN in 1988 and PUMPKIN KID in 1992. She also took two Lenington All-American Awards for daylilies which grow well over most of the nation: YESTERDAY MEMORIES in 1986 followed by LULLABY BABY in 1988. For the best lavender daylily she received the James E. Marsh Award in 1989 for GRACEFUL EYE.

Finally, it is significant that for many years the Spalding daylilies have appeared regularly on the annual Award of Merit list—a steak-and-potatoes Big Ten of Awards & Honors.

ED GROVATT · 1981

New Jersey hybridizer Ed Grovatt is so closely associated with the daylily ED MURRAY it is easy to forget that he was well-known for his big, clear yellow daylilies. They are especially suited to northern gardens in that they are healthy, hardy plants. DOT GROVATT, AMY GROVATT, and EMMA GRIFFING are a sampling of the more popular yellow introductions.

Then there was the "Jersey" series: JERSEY BEACON, JERSEY TOUGHIE—both reds—and JERSEY FLAMINGO, a bright pink. All of the above won Honorable Mentions.

At the Pittsburgh convention in 1978, Mr. Grovatt won the President's Cup for his BERT MURRAY, a large, copper-colored flower with a triangular form.

When ED MURRAY was introduced in 1973 it was a sensation. The dark, velvety-red small flower was absolutely sunfast. Even the green throat held. Furthermore, it had wavy ruffles, a flat, open bloom, and it seemed full enough for its day. It received

photo by Harvey Horne

5-34. *Ed Grovatt of New Jersey, touring in 1975.*

the Stout Medal, the Annie T. Giles Medal, and the Lenington All-American Award.

Not everyone liked it. A few critiques condemned its height which was rather tall (though well-branched) for a small flower. Then came the knockout blow for hybridizers. It was sterile.

Fortune intervened in the name of Jack Romine. This fine gentleman from Walnut Creek, California, was an early proponent of colchicine treatment and was a chief supplier of chimeral pollen in those days when it was considered "raw gold." He later sold converted plants or sometimes simply shared them as befitted his generous nature.

In addition, Jack Romine hybridized with small flowers. Tetraploid small flowers, of course. And so when ED MURRAY came along with all its superior esthetic qualities, Jack managed to convert it. The most exciting part of the conversion was that Tet ED MURRAY was pollen fertile! Not lustily so, but it did prove itself capable of procreation.

Characteristically, Mr. Romine shared a piece of the new tet with William and Eleanor Lachman of Massachusetts. Later, Dr. Lachman reported an initial problem with germination and the final successful workaround:

. . . After the seeds were harvested and dried, however, all of them became very shriveled like raisins. This was very discouraging as we usually discard

5-35.
*Clarke Yancey,
hybridizing in his
garden, 1972.*

photo by Tom Wise

such shriveled seed on the assumption they do not germinate. About that time while perusing an old Journal we happened upon an article written by Jack Romine in which he reported that some wizened seed proved to be viable (Hem. J. 23 #2: 83 1969).

Thereupon, last September we treated our ED MURRAY hybrid seed with Arasan® dust and placed them in a petri dish on wet paper toweling and imbibed them with water for about a week when a majority of the seeds became quite swollen. Then about one-third of the seed coat and the thin endosperm membrane was removed from the micropylar end of the seed with a sharp knife as described by Griesbach and Voth (Bot. Gaz. 118: 223-237: 1957). Seeds were then planted in a Moist Jiffy-Mix and within a few days about 50% of our treasure germinated.

Such was the beginning of a happy ending.

Clarke Yancey - 1982

Clarke Yancey, a modest man from Woodbine, Georgia, was once asked how he got started in hybridizing. He explained that he bought a whole collection of daylilies from H. M. Russell of Spring, Texas, for $14.00. "We really splurged," Clarke said. "We had saved up for a trip and couldn't go, so we bought daylilies instead.

Now, after more than 30 years of hybridizing he doesn't claim to have found blue at the end of the rainbow, but the popularity of his daylilies attests to more than moderate success.

Although blue would have been nice, it was never his intent to specialize. "I just cross the best with the best and wait for the results."

In the beginning, wide petals eluded him. "I did get some nice colors in the early days, but they were all narrow petaled."

His first break came when he obtained breeding stock from John Weisner in Florida. He crossed these seedlings with his own stock, but still the petals were narrow—with one notable exception: LP-11-65. This breakthrough not only got him away from the narrow petals, but it gave him some of his best, clearest colors up to that point. LP-11-65 was a complex cross of (((FRANCES FAY x LYRIC) X (SHOW GIRL X GAY ORCHID)) X ((REFLECTION x (GAY ORCHID X SATIN GLASS))). (The path to glory is never simple.)

From this one lavender seedling came some of Clarke Yancey's most memorable work: the delicate pink TENDER LOVE, one of the best late blooming daylilies available, CHERRY FESTIVAL, a rose red, and ELIZABETH YANCEY, a pale textured pink.

Mr. Yancey soon began keeping accurate records and line breeding, but he never hesitated to make outcrosses when something interesting caught his fancy.

Two of Clarke Yancey's introductions should be noted because of their exceptional color—or lack of it in the case of GENTLE SHEPHERD. This daylily is at least in the race for the nearest-to-white daylily that has been produced. And the smaller CHRISTMAS IS is surely the most distinctive red on the market to date, owing to its exceptionally

photo by Mary Gage

5-36. *Ury G. Winniford, serious about his hybridizing; less so about himself.*

5-37.
*Oscie B. Whatley
with Alabama hybridizer
Sarah Sikes.*

photo by Frances Gatlin

wide, uniquely patterned green throat. This has been converted and used hopefully by many hybridizers, but the original version maintains the edge for pure distinction.

Ury G. Winniford - 1983

Ury Winniford claims that he can't remember when he got into daylilies, but it started with a gift plant of HYPERION. This led him to the Russell establishment in Spring, Texas.

Daylilies of that time were narrow petaled and bloomed out rather quickly. A few years later Mr. Winniford visited Lucille Williamson and saw his first daylilies with improved form. He attempted to get this in his own daylilies by crossing the Russell purchases, but the results were disappointing.

A visit to the Hughes Garden near Mansfield, Texas, started him on the right track. There he obtained a seedling with much wider petals than he had ever seen. He set goals and started keeping records. Wider petals were the first order of the day. Later came shorter scapes, branching, and high bud count. In the later part of his career he has worked toward different colors, heavy substance, and ruffling. He has not specialized in any one size, color, size, or ploidy.

Chief among his varied accomplishments are: BERTIE FERRIS - Stout Medal in 1980, Donn Fischer Award in 1973; SQUEAKY - Donn Fischer Award in 1974; and POJO, a yellow double that took the Ida Munson in 1977. At the 1975 convention in Dallas, many visitors were taken with the rose-dusted yellow BRUTUS, a large, recurved flower. More recent introductions have been PEGGY HAMMEL and ZULU QUEEN.

Oscie B. Whatley - 1984

Born and raised in Texas, Oscie Whatley has lived in the St. Louis, Missouri, area for many years. A favorite aunt was responsible for his long involvement with daylilies.

This is a hybridizer who lives and breathes his hobby. Someone once wrote of him that he has integrity as it applies to "hybridizer." That would be putting too narrow a scope on the application, but the point is well taken. It is true that he puts his name only on what he considers to be his best work and does not indulge in overstatement.

A trademark of the Whatley daylilies has always been flat flower form. As he states, "One form which still turns me on is what I call super flatness. It opens very early and reliably, even in unfavorable weather. JAKARTA put this characteristic into many a yellow seedling and the influence has spread to other colors such as red (ABEX) and melon (FEMME OSAGE)."

His yellows first brought Oscie to the attention of daylily growers. Most of his yellows have a strong "carrying power" that makes them useful in the landscape; he selects for this quality. Yellow continues to be an important line. After JAKARTA (Award of Merit, 1975) came LAHAINA, MOLOKAI (Award of Merit, 1984), POTOSI, CALEDONIA, YEBIT, and TUSCAN. The older beige-yellow CHARBONIER is still a showpiece when in full bloom and displaying its very flat, 5-inch, full flowers.

Ruffling and fringe has been added to the flat forms. In Oscie's experience, the knobby fringe or lacing, as opposed to ruffles, is a tetraploid characteristic. His late-flowering YUMA is an example of an extremely fringed daylily.

The St. Louis hybridizers of the 1960s enthusiastically endorsed the new wave of tetraploids. Harold Harris, George Pettus, and Oscie Whatley all mastered the techniques of conversion. Oscie is still converting diploid stock for himself and others. His more recent red line is from induced CHRISTMAS IS (Yancey) and induced SILOAM RED TOY (Henry, P.). He converted SILOAM MEDALLION to obtain large, ruffled yellows such as ISOSCELES, CRUMPLE, and SOLAR MUSIC.

As a life member of AHS, Oscie Whatley prefers to leave the organizational activities to others, but he is always ready to share through writing or conversation his philosophy, insight, and practical knowledge on the subject of hybridizing. This is his true love.

Pauline Henry - 1985

The "Siloam" prefix is familiar in the daylily world. Growers quickly come to recognize such registrations as belonging to Pauline Henry of Siloam Springs, Arkansas.

In 1993, Pauline Henry won the Stout Medal for her smooth pink SILOAM DOUBLE CLASSIC. This is interesting in that her fame lies with another class, not doubles, and although she has successfully diversified in recent years, she will always be associated with exquisitely formed small and miniature daylilies, especially those with an eye pattern. The popularity of this line has earned her other major awards:

The Donn Fischer (miniature) Award for SILOAM JUNE BUG, SILOAM RED TOY, SILOAM TEE TINY, SILOAM BERTIE FERRIS, and SILOAM GRACE STAMILE.

The Annie T. Giles (small flower) Award for SILOAM VIRGINIA HENSON, SILOAM JIM COOPER and SILOAM MERLE KENT. The latter also received two President's Cup awards.

These little ones have earned recognition in other categories. SILOAM TEE TINY was voted the James E. Marsh award for best lavender or purple daylily while both SILOAM BERTIE FERRIS and SILOAM VIRGINIA HENSON received the Don C. Stevens Award for best eyed daylily.

She also won the Ida Munson double award for her SILOAM DOUBLE CLASSIC.

Occasionally she has produced large-flowered yellows. Her SILOAM MAMA was a popular introduction in this class.

She has shown a talent for winning awards that equals her prowess as a hybridizer. It would be impossible to list all her awards here.

Pauline Henry has never been one to keep records. Other hybridizers have picked up her work and tracked the results. One of her most famous parents is SILOAM VIRGINIA HENSON, not in its original form but as converted to tetraploid. A number of hybridizers have had outstanding results with it.

photo by Darrel Apps

5-38. *Pauline Henry of Siloam Springs, Arkansas*

David Kirchhoff - 1986

In 1987 when David Kirchhoff assumed the responsibilities of RVP for Region 12, his predecessor Justine Lee "introduced" him with these words:

David, whose first spoken word was "flower," is a fourth generation horticulturist. Born in Sanford, Florida, in 1942, he is a hybridizer and follows in his late father's footsteps. Along with his partner, Morton Morss, he operates Daylily World in Sanford. In addition to managing the affairs of Daylily World, he is employed as the personnel manager for an interiorscape company in Florida.

The wonder is that David has found time to develop so many interests. Early on, a career in music fell by the wayside as he became heavily involved with AHS, daylilies, and hybridizing. He continues to contribute many hours to the organizational side of the Society, but hybridizing is his true master. The effort has borne fruit.

In 1991, David's golden yellow double BETTY WOODS received the coveted Stout Medal.

Doubles have held a keen interest with David, ever since he noticed the trait showing up on some of his father's seedlings. He began to cross them, with the eventual result of NAGASAKI, a cream, pink, and lavender. The line passed through several way stations—CABBAGE FLOWER, COSMIC TREASURE, and other interesting preludes—before it came to rest at BETTY WOODS.

Progress in doubles continued unabated. A deep red double, STROKE OF MIDNIGHT was the second Kirchhoff cultivar to receive the Ida Munson Award for doubles. (BETTY WOODS was the first and CABBAGE FLOWER the third.) IMPERIAL DRAGON, HOLY MACKEREL, and LOHENGRIN are other reds that have been enthusiastically received.

Tetraploid doubles have been a challenge, but David is at the head of his class.

He has been working with both tetraploid and diploid single flowers. Among his tet line he has produced such standouts as the Award of Merit MING PORCELAIN, a round, pastel blend; and ED KIRCHHOFF, a ruffled, brilliant yellow. Another notable tetraploid has been the burgundy red

5-39. *David Kirchhoff, successful hybridizer and ambassador for daylilies.*

ZINFANDEL which won the James E. Marsh award for best purple or lavender daylily. The daylily is, in fact, an odd choice for that award, being nearer to red than purple. However, it is an exceptional red with bluish undertones.

In the diploid field, David's first introduction, JEAN WOOTON, was to receive an Award of Merit eight years later. Another heralded diploid is his BETTE DAVIS EYES which received the Don C. Stevens Award for best eyed daylily.

Finally, less is more, so the saying goes; and there could scarcely be a better small package than CHORUS LINE which has it all—branching, bud count, adaptability, and a beautiful countenance. The face is an unblemished pink, the throat is green surrounded by a subtle rose band, and the form is just right. This won another Award of Merit for David as well as the Annie T. Giles Award for small flowers. In 1994, the board of directors recognized its broad appeal and adaptability by voting it the Lenington All-American Award.

Van Sellers - 1987

It might be said that Van Sellers has been more interested in other hybridizers' daylilies than his own. If D. R. McKeithan was the Great Evaluator

photo by Harvey Horne

5-40. *Van Sellers, a modern-day Great Evaluator.*

of the 1950s, Van Sellers is his counterpart of today. A major difference is that Mr. McKeithan went to the daylilies while Van brings the daylilies to his own Iron Gate Gardens for study. He buys stock from growers all over the country, large and small. Who could resist playing in this genetic pool?

Van once wrote that red was his favorite color. The choice seems to suit him. And he has had some success in producing the plush-like RED JOY and the more flamboyant BIG APPLE that is a part of everybody's list or garden. Several intermediate, less memorable steps marked the way. As he predicted, red proved to be a challenge. BIG APPLE received an Award of Merit in 1992.

His success with the near-whites came sooner. IRON GATE GLACIER and IRON GATE ICEBERG rose quickly to the prestigious Award of Merit. These triumphs were followed by WHITE TEMPTATION.

The Sellers large yellow daylilies have also garnered several awards. FROZEN JADE received the L. Ernest Plouf Award for fragrance in 1981 and the Richard C. Peck Award for best tetraploid daylily in 1982. It has an Award of Merit to its credit as well. BEAUTY TO BEHOLD, a large lemon self, continues to bring in honors—most recently the 1993 Lenington All-American Award.

Other Sellers daylilies of assorted colors that have found a place in many gardens are TOO MARVELOUS, a pale pink-yellow blend which received an Award of Merit in 1989; PINK MONDAY, a vigorous tet; SECOND GLANCE, intense canteloupe melon self; and EXOTIC ECHO, a cream-pink small flower with an unusual double eye ring of lavender and burgundy. This received the Annie T. Giles Award in 1993, followed by an Award of Merit in 1994.

Kenneth G. Durio, Jr. - 1988

Some regions encourage competition/progress among their hybridizers by special awards for seedlings or unintroduced cultivars. In Region 13, it is the Emma Middlebrook Award, and in a hotbed of hybridizers, Ken Durio has won it four times:

PINK HURRICANE - 1972
FRED GERALD - 1978
FRANK GLADNEY - 1981
MA - 1984

Probably the most familiar of these is FRANK GLADNEY, a very large, textured, coral-pink tetraploid which later added an Award of Merit to its list of credits.

Ken was not unlike countless other hem growers in that his first daylilies were Russell cultivars. And, like others, he later found something better. In his case, the awakening was spurred by a visit to the Simon Nursery in Lafayette, Louisiana.

He later became acquainted with Edna Spalding who had begun converting diploids to tetraploids. With the purchase of a lavender Spalding tet seedling and the "Crestwood" (Fay) series acquired from MacMillan, Ken began his dual program of hybridizing diploids and tetraploids.

The first good parent Ken produced was pale yellow INEZ CLARY. This was crossed with Edna Spalding's Stout Medal recipient, LAVENDER FLIGHT. Eventually, the line led to Ken's own 1983 Stout Award for MY BELLE.

Although it missed winning the Stout Medal, JOAN SENIOR has achieved as much if not more popularity. Award of Merit winner and the 1990 winner of the Lenington All-American Award, it is a round, recurved, near-white daylily.

Other large-flowered introductions that have become popular are DARRELL, a 7-inch, creped yellow, and BYRAN PAUL, a deep red with a thin white edge around the petals.

Along the way, Ken became interested in doubles. In 1982, PAPA GULINO, a pink and rose blend, was voted the annual Ida Munson Award for best double. It happened also to be a *tetraploid* double which was almost an exclusive class at the time. He has continued work in this field.

Ken and Belle Durio have a large family and at one time most of them were dabbing pollen at home. Now only Dalton and Albert are working at the nursery. Both are hybridizing and introducing cultivars of their own.

Charlie Pierce - 1989

Charlie Pierce of Mobile, Alabama, died on the eve of the awards presentation at which he was to receive the Bertrand Farr Medal. He was at the peak of his career as a hybridizer.

Mr. Pierce was known for his modesty, high standards, and integrity. One story has to do with BEVERLY ANN. It was a beautiful, light rose pink and several admirers who saw it in his garden placed advance orders. As the plant developed, Mr. Pierce decided that it did not meet his exacting standards. Rather than market a daylily he considered to be less than perfect, he withdrew it and refunded the full value to those who had ordered. BEVERLY ANN later became a valuable parent, but he did not consider it a finished flower.

His daylilies are all diploid, in the large-flower class, and they are studies in pink, cream, yellow, and pastel blends. The form is always classic and refined.

The first great success was FAIRY TALE PINK. It broke many records on its way up the ladder. A perennial favorite on the Popularity Poll, it also won the President's Cup and the Stout Medal. Despite the name, it was not as pink as some of Mr. Pierce's later introductions.

In 1992, a pale lavender pink without the melon cast of FAIRY TALE PINK won the Stout Medal. This was the incomparable BARBARA MITCHELL. A little larger, too, it is beautifully formed with a heavy, ribbed texture and ruffles. As a clump or an individual bloom, it attracts attention.

5-41. Belle and Ken Durio. She is the 'My Belle,' he the winner.

Other Pierce daylilies that have received the Award of Merit are CREATIVE ART and ROSE EMILY. After Mr. Pierce's death, a seedling was selected and released under the name CHARLIE PIERCE MEMORIAL.

Lucille Guidry - 1990

The feat of capturing two consecutive Stout Medals is a rarity that has been accomplished only twice in AHS history. Carl Milliken's long-standing record was tied by a much beloved lady from Louisiana— Lucille Guidry. Her Stout awards were for JANET GAYLE (1986) and BECKY LYNN (1987).

Mrs. Guidry's career began with her assignment to W. B. MacMillan as his nurse. Clarence Crochet extracted this story:

Lucille Guidry became a regular nurse for the MacMillans in 1969 when Peggy Mac became invalid after a household accident. After Mrs. MacMillan's death, Lucille continued nursing by taking care of MacMillan during the day. It was then that she became acquainted with daylilies and especially with

photo by Earlene Garber

5-42. Lucille Guidry, a case of the student surpassing the master.

hybridizing. Mr. Mac would be brought into the garden at first in a wheelchair, to supervise the hybridizing. From his wheelchair, he showed Lucille how to hybridize by pointing out plants with his walking stick and having her place pollen on the selected seedlings. Later, when he became well enough, he managed to walk in the garden with Lucille and continued to direct the hybridizing at a close hand. He showed Lucille the fundamentals of hybridizing—even how to make a cross tag.

In the beginning, Mr. Mac gave Lucille his discarded plants to landscape her yard. As her interest and knowledge increased, he named a daylily for her and gave her a plant to grow at home. Next he gave her a JUMBO RED followed by many others. She began bringing pollen of AGGIE SELLERS home to use on a pink seedling. The cross produced JANET GAYLE. She brought MacMillan a bloom to see and asked for his opinion. He replied, "Lady, you've already outdone me with this one."

Form has always been paramount with Mrs. Guidry. For her to look at a daylily twice, it must have wide overlapping segments, ruffling, and firm substance.

She works with a variety of colors. There are rich rose pinks such as BECKY LYNN, honeyed shades epitomized by LITTLE DEEKE and WHISKY ON ICE, and even purple, represented by the double BRENT GABRIEL. She has introduced a number of interesting blends.

Her awards tell the story. In addition to her two Stout Medals, she has received at least five Awards of Merit. One of these, SMOKY MOUNTAIN AUTUMN, has appeared with regularity on the Popularity Poll and is an unusual dark pink blend with a lavender halo. Another, GOLDEN SCROLL, is a soft tangerine rather than gold and is also fragrant. It received the Plouf Award.

The Guidry family works as a team. From the beginning, her late husband, Gabriel, helped with the beds. Later, son Davis organized the marketing.

BRYANT MILLIKAN · 1991

Another stickler for form was Bryant Millikan of Indianapolis. Several years ago he was happily growing roses and iris when a friend thrust upon him some older daylilies. Instead of seeing their lack of appeal, Bryant looked upon them as plants in need of help, whereupon he set about to improve them. He joined AHS to learn more. Soon he acquired SABIE (MacMillan) and began hybridizing with it. As a direct result of that purchase, BROCADED GOWN made its appearance in Bryant's seedling patch and went on to win the Stout Medal for him in 1989. The actual cross that produced BROCADED GOWN was SABIE X BUTTERMILK SKY (MacMillan).

BROCADED GOWN has been used extensively as a parent, in conjunction with various outcrosses. Bryant frequently made use of favored breeding stock from other hybridizers. Examples: CHARBONIER (Whatley), FAIRY CHARM (Jablonski), WYNNSON (Criswell), and LITTLE INFANT (Monette).

In the beginning, Bryant concentrated on diploid yellows with considerable success. Some of his more popular in this class were TOM COLLINS, MARBLE FAUN, VIDEO, GREEN EYED LADY, and HOOP SKIRT.

He later decided to branch out with tetraploids. With the help of such parents as JAMES MARSH

(Marsh-Klehm), DOUGLAS DALE, DRAGON LORE, GENTLE DRAGON (all Peck), and ANNIE GOLIGHTLY (Hughes), he produced his own line of red tetraploids. Two of the most notable are STOP SIGN and BLOOD SPOT. He did some work with red dips as well, e.g., CARLOTTA, a red and cherry blend.

Another line involving LITTLE INFANT and Sellers' WHITE TEMPTATION produced good near whites such as SNOWED IN and ASPEN. Shortly before his death in 1995, he was searching for better substance in the "whites."

He considered pink to be the most challenging color, and was also working in that area. Perhaps he had already planted the seed of his dreams.

STEVE MOLDOVAN · 1992

After 35 years of daylily breeding, Steve Moldovan has experienced a role reversal. As a teenager he was a protege of Orville Fay and a close-up admirer of the great Chicago-area hybridizers. Now, attrition having depleted their ranks, Steve has senior status as a Midwest breeder. He is attempting to pass on some valuable lessons learned from the great ones and from his own experience.

At the Minneapolis RVP Interview, with Steve Moldovan as the subject, he was asked about his famous STRUTTER'S BALL. The question unleashed a torrent of memories. In 1958, he said, his mad passion was purple. Easy if you are an iris breeder as Steve was, but daylilies? There just weren't any true purples.

There was also the problem of hardiness for northern breeders. In the end, the two divergent paths merged into one happy ending. But let Steve tell the story:

> When I started daylilies, I grew northern varieties because I'd heard that southern evergreens would die for us. So I bred dormant with dormant. I remember sending some of my initial seedlings down to southern Florida to be grown and tested to see how they'd grow, and they didn't! I was crushed, of course. I went down there and said, "What am I going to do?"
>
> I started a program of crossing northern things with southern things. I took the best from the North, and at that time it was Orville Fay, David Hall, and others, and I took the best from the South. At that

5-43. *Steve Moldovan, fierce advocate of breeding for vigor and disease resistance.*

photo by Harvey Horne

time it was Edna Spalding who had pinks and lavenders. I combined them. Through several generations I selected the purple color, and that's STRUTTER'S BALL. The final cross was my line of purple breeding, which contains southern and northern, and I went back to the South to my friend, Bill Munson, who had a very fine purple in his southern lines. So it's a combination of North and South.

For two reasons, STRUTTER'S BALL is an important daylily for me and for my goals. Number one, it is a purple which has superb branching, both in the North and the South. The color is very sun resistant. None of them are perfect, but this one is pretty good. And it reblooms both in the North and in the South.

His passion for purple has given rise to a much-expanded class—a hybridizing boon to himself and other hybridizers. His introductions of ROYAL WATERMARK, MAGIC ROBE, and the landmark EMPRESS SEAL have been integrated into many lavender and purple tetraploid lines.

Steve himself does not believe in line breeding past a generation or two. It is part of his philosophy and plan for maintaining (or restoring) vigor to the daylily. (See his comments under "Concerns of Tomorrow," Chapter 8.)

Steve maintains that the old "rule" against crossing dissimilar colors is invalid with tetraploids. Some of his best things came through a wild cross. At the tetraploid level, he says, anything is possible. One wonders if he had AVANTE GARDE in mind when he made this observation. It is bitoned, bordered, *and* eyed!

His pinks have been winners. DANCING SHIVA became an instant hit after it displayed well at a convention. Steve cites LOVE GODDESS as his most influential parent. It has greatly advanced

photo by Frances Gatlin

5-44. *Enman and Frances Joiner, tour-garden hosts at the 1989 Savannah convention.*

his work in pinks. He is outcrossing the beautiful lavender-pink MARISKA to other colors. VERA BIAGLOW is a popular rose pink.

What is Steve looking for now? Rebloom! The South has it. He wants it for the North.

ENMAN R. JOINER - 1993

In company with hundreds of others, Enman Joiner ordered a collection of daylilies from Russell Gardens from an advertisement in the *Popular Gardening Magazine.* Unlike the majority of those buyers, he rapidly turned the collection into 10,000 seedlings. He kept only two. One was a rose that showed doubling tendencies. This trait so intrigued him that he made double-flowering daylilies a primary objective. It remains so today.

In time, his line breeding for doubles led to grassy foliage, so he began searching for a cultivar that would put vigor into his line. The chosen one was DOUBLE EVA, a large, extremely vigorous evergreen double hybridized by Kirby Sutton in Florida. To this he added Lucille Guidry's sometimes-double NATHAN CARROLL to improve color. It was a long path to FRANCES JOINER, but interesting things happened along the way.

For several years Mr. Joiner gained more recognition inside his region than out of it. He won four Region 5 Hybridizer Awards and six Achievement Medals. Then the 1989 AHS National Convention was staged in Savannah and visitors got an eyeful of what 25 years of devotion to a "hobby" can do. A large grouping of FRANCES JOINER, a beautifully formed double in shades of pink, honey, and rose, easily swung the vote for the President's Cup. It was his second such award; the first was for SAVANNAH MOON in 1970.

One of the most unusual large flowers is PAT MERCER, described as Mars Orange. It first came to the attention of the daylily-growing population on account of its extended-bloom habit. It is tender—a plant for warmer climates.

Mr. Joiner received Awards of Merit for SAVANNAH DAWN, PAT MERCER, NELL JESSUP, BANGLE, and FRANCES JOINER. All are large single flowers excepting the double FRANCES JOINER.

photo by Harvey Horne

5-45. *Kate Carpenter, displaying the 1984 Lambert Award, regional recognition for her LAKE NORMAN SUNSET.*

In 1993 FRANCES JOINER received the Ida Munson Award for best double daylily voted by the Awards & Honors Judges.

In 1993, VANILLA FLUFF won the Plouf Award for the fragrance of its creamy yellow double bloom. It is a big flower on strong, tall scapes.

Enman Joiner continues to explore new fields. He is now into tetraploids. A red tet double recently passed its first test on the show table.

KATE CARPENTER - 1994

On the shores of Lake Norman in North Carolina, buffered by a massive sea wall, lies the "wonderscape" of hybridizer/artist-in-residence Kate Carpenter. This garden has lured many visitors and photographers to its fabulous collection of daylilies and hosta. Artfully set amid pines and palms, the scene is one of spectacular beauty.

Kate the hybridizer carries her designing talents a step beyond the landscape. She has created some of the most stylishly different daylilies available in the 1980s, the decade that might be considered her zenith. Her volume of output has never been prolific; it is quality and distinction that brought her fame as a hybridizer.

She has not specialized in a particular form or color. Some of her artistic forms, such as the popular LAKE NORMAN SPIDER, PEACOCK MAIDEN, and older SWIRLING WATER are in the lavender-purple class. These are not true spiders, but their distinctive forms always attract attention in the garden.

Some of her most popular introductions have been unusual blends. LAKE NORMAN SUNSET mixes pink, yellow, and everything in-between on a heavily textured surface. NEW SERIES has some of the same colors and looks entirely different. Multi-colored rings surround a wide green throat on a large pink daylily. UNIQUE STYLE is smaller, very uniform and has the pink pattern sprayed atop a yellow base.

Following her success with pink blends, Kate produced a limited number of excellent smooth, ruffled pinks such as SUE ROTHBAUER and HARBORGATE.

Large yellow daylilies of the "Allen" family, namely ALEC ALLEN and then BLAKE ALLEN have won for Kate two President's Cups.

5-46. *Lee Gates, photo 1994. A Landscape Architect and hybridizer especially noted for his vigorous red tetraploids.*

Her accomplishments have merited notable honors, including five Awards of Merit and the Don C. Stevens Award.

LEE GATES - 1995

As a Landscape Architect by profession, Lee Gates drifted quite naturally into designing the "furniture" for his trade. Daylilies were an obvious choice for fitting out the garden rooms of Mobile, Alabama. By the time he moved to Louisiana, daylilies were the whole room.

It was a colorful room. From the start, Lee worked for clear colors and he has produced them across the spectrum. He has bred for full form as well as color, using the best available parents to reach his goals.

Reds have been his greatest success. They are well known and well grown from Louisiana to Pittsburgh. Northern growers have proclaimed most of Lee's reds to be remarkably hardy and vigorous. It was at a northern convention—Detroit—that CHARLES JOHNSTON took the President's Cup.

Two other hardy reds in this color class have won Awards of Merit: deep red SEDUCTOR and the brighter SCARLET ORBIT. By 1994, the newer JOVIAL had climbed to a position of runner-up to the Award of Merit.

The near-white MONICA MARIE may be Lee's most important parent to date. This beautifully formed, 5-inch daylily has been used extensively as a parent. It is another Award of Merit recipient.

Lee has developed several worthwhile doubles. ALMOST INDECENT is a delectable blend of lavender and cream. The name typifies the hybridizer's puckish sense of humor—not, surely, his character. Other eyebrow raisers have crept into his repertoire of lovelies, so one has to assume that the home of SEDUCTOR and SEDUCTRESS would be at least stimulating if not Altogether Indecent.

It was Lee's original intention to concentrate on tetraploids. To this purpose, he used conversions of the best diploids. Unfortunately, some were not stable, and this resulted in an all-too-common problem of the time: a few diploids registered as tetraploids. When questions of ploidy were raised by hybridizers attempting to make crosses with these suspect plants, Lee hired a laboratory to do chromosome counts on his own daylilies as well as those of other hybridizers. The study was cut short by personnel upsets at the laboratory, but preliminary results confirmed the fact of diploidy in some of Lee's stock. Fortunately, the reds were tetraploid. Tests further uncovered other cases of misregistered ploidy from various sources before the ill-fated study was aborted.

This experience, unhappy as it may have been, served to call attention to a potential problem that is inherent in first-generation crosses with converted material. The problem should recede as the tetraploid gene pool expands. Meanwhile, hybridizers have become more alert to the possible masquerade. We can thank hybridizers such as Lee who cared enough to strip the mask away.

Chapter 6

Registrations

Quite simply, the fundamental objective of registration is to strive for the stability of names.
HARRY TUGGLE

The Role of the American Plant Life Society

HE AMERICAN HEMEROCALLIS SOCIETY had scarcely gained its birthright when the first compilation of *Hemerocallis* registrations went to press. Obviously, the young Society was not in a position at that time to have initiated a major publication.

DESCRIPTIVE CATALOG OF HEMEROCALLIS CLONES: 1893–1948

Credit for the *Descriptive Catalog of Hemerocallis Clones: 1893–1948* goes to the American Plant Life Society, an organization whose primary focus in those days was on amaryllis and daylilies. The editor of its scientific journal, *Herbertia*, was Hamilton P. Traub who, along with other APLS members, later contributed important work to the American Hemerocallis Society. While the APLS underwrote the publication cost of this first catalog of registrations, the newly formed Hemerocallis Society participated in its sponsorship. It was compiled by J. B. S. Norton, Sc.D., M. Frederick Stuntz, and W. R. Ballard, B.S., and published by the American Plant Life Society in Stanford, California, 1949.

The catalog was a dream of Dr. Traub, who followed the work to completion. With no ongoing registration process established, collecting the first records was a formidable task. Compilers relied upon lists published by Dr. Stout in *Herbertia* and elsewhere, the manuscript list of Dr. L. H. MacDaniels, and a card index contributed by Elmer Claar.

That the catalog includes coded color descriptions at all is due to the influence of M. Frederick Stuntz. The original plan did not call for descriptions, but Mr. Stuntz volunteered to add them by adapting for *Hemerocallis* the system used by the American Iris Society.

By November 1, 1948, the catalog had recorded accumulated totals of 2,452 clones and 166 breeders. Already, prophetic minds were voicing concerns. In his foreword to the catalog, Dr. Traub warns:

> It cannot be too strongly emphasized that the publication of the name and description of a new plant clone and its distribution is a *very serious matter*. In the first place, the gardener should not be deluged with inferior clones that will soon be discarded. Secondly, the standing of the breeder is partly gauged by the percentage of his introductions that stand the test of time. . . . *If the clone does not survive in public favor, the recorded name and description in most cases represent just so much dead timber* [his italics].

As with future *Check Lists* to be published by the American Hemerocallis Society, the editors of the *Descriptive Catalog of Hemerocallis Clones* made a

---

THE AMERICAN PLANT LIFE SOCIETY BECOMES THE INTERNATIONAL BULB SOCIETY

The American Plant Life Society, not unlike the AHS, has undergone two name changes since its formation in 1933 as the American Amaryllis Society. Shortly thereafter it became the American Plant Life Society (APLS). Most of the references in this book pertain to the long period of incorporation under that name.

In January of 1991, the APLS again changed its name and is at this writing incorporated as the International Bulb Society. Throughout its history, the society's publication has been titled *Herbertia*.

determined effort to adhere to the International Rules of Botanical Nomenclature.

AHS IS MADE INTERNATIONAL REGISTRY FOR DAYLILIES

In the decade that was to follow before the AHS published its own compilation, annual registration reports were being printed in the AHS *Yearbooks* and AHS Newsletters. *Check List Supplements* were introduced at a later date.

By 1955, the Society had been granted the role of International Registry for Daylilies.

A procession of registrars marched through those early years. The first on record was M. Frederick Stuntz who had assisted with the *Descriptive Catalog* published by the American Plant Life Association. His remarks, found in this book among the charter members, give some indication of his devotion to his task. William E. Monroe was later to characterize the first AHS registrar as the most accurate, precise man he had ever met. Unfortunately, those traits, so eminently suited to managing records, proved to be a hindrance in dealing with the human element.

Two years later, Olive Hindman accepted a board appointment as Mr. Stuntz's replacement. This was another short term, lasting only one year until an obliging Wilmer Flory added two years as registrar to his long record of service to the Society.

He was followed by Harry Tuggle, a most intelligent, if somewhat impatient, young botanist. Two years were quite enough for him. After his work on the first *Check List*, he went on to other things and left the next 32 years to William E. Monroe.

HEMEROCALLIS CHECK LIST 1893 TO JULY 1, 1957

The first *Hemerocallis Check List* published by the AHS was compiled by M. Frederick Stuntz, Paul D. Voth, Earl A. Holl, Wilmer B. Flory, Harry I. Tuggle, Jr., and the new AHS registrar, William E. Monroe. The foreword, written by the irascible Harry Tuggle and reproduced here in part, is interesting:

> . . .The number of named daylilies has approached the dimensions of atomic fallout—from 2,452 names in the 1949 catalog, to over 7,000 in this work. We

6-1.
Hamilton P. Traub, editor of the APLS DESCRIPTIVE LIST OF HEMEROCALLIS CLONES— *1893-1948.*

should not be proud of this large increase, for only a minority of the additional clones have been of lasting value. However, we are indeed proud that we have kept pace with this tidal wave of registrations and introductions.

The American Hemerocallis Society, Inc. began its registration service in 1947 in cooperation with the American Plant Life Society, when we were a young and relatively regional organization. We assisted in compiling the 1949 catalog, and since that date with the growth of the society, we have assumed full registration authority for the genus, on both a national and international level. Our petition to the 1955 International Horticultural Congress to serve as International Registration Authority for *Hemerocallis* was accepted and approved. In cooperation with the American Horticultural Council, Inc., we now operate under the aegis of the International Horticultural Congress and under the provisional International Code of Nomenclature of Cultivated Plants (1952) as supplemented by the 1955 Code of Registration Procedure.

The primary purpose of registration is to scrupulously avoid application of the same name to more than one clone. . . . While registrations continue unabated at the rate of five to six hundred per year, it is neither our function nor desire to limit registration. Testing or determination of value is not a function of registration. . . . Quite simply, the fundamental objective of registration is to strive for the stability of names.

Note: In his own account to follow, William E. Monroe, who oversaw the printing of this work, gives a humorous apologia for its errors. Mr. Tuggle also had something to say about that:

> The immediate need for a checklist* at this time outweighs any argument for desirability of waiting until we might publish a more perfect work. Since 1938, additions have been scattered throughout nine issues of our Yearbook and six issues of our Newsletter. . . .
>
> In this age of mass production, mass markets, and mass entertainment, our daylily hybridizers have not failed to follow the trend. A strong dose of some potent elixir is needed to calm the prolific deluge of registrations and introductions. No-one can tell a mother that one of her children has dirty ears, but there is no place for maternalism or "momism," in *Hemerocallis* evaluation. We hope that this large volume with its almost eight thousand entries will shock our hybridizers into the realization that multitudinous introductions are of no import—that only quality counts. There is no room for insularity in the hybridizing garden.
>
> If this checklist serves in any degree as a deterrent to indiscriminate naming, and encourages more objective evaluation before registration, our work shall be doubly rewarding.
>
> —HARRY I. TUGGLE, JR., 1957

Following the completion of the first American Hemerocallis Society *Check List* in 1957, and following a dream of Bill E. Monroe, future registrations lists were bound in annual supplements so that published records were no longer scattered thither and yon. Until 1970 these supplements were titled *Hemerocallis Clones*, with the appropriate date following. Thenceforth, to comply more closely with the definitions in the eyes of the International Code of Nomenclature, the supplements were titled *Hemerocallis Cultivars*.

---

*Here we find *checklist* spelled as one word—in direct conflict with the author's previous assertion (p. 63) that it wasn't done in those days. Well, hardly ever. Harry Tuggle had an eye to the future, whether it concerned spelling or registrations.

A Color Chart

COLOR DESCRIPTIONS that appear in recent *Check Lists* and elsewhere have been lampooned as inaccurate, inscrutable, overly imaginative, and inordinately hopeful. Contemporary critics have recommended the adoption of a color chart. It may come as a surprise to newer members that neither the complaint nor the proposed solution is new.

The first combined *Check List* made use of a color classification chart in its coded system, the very existence for which credit is due the first AHS registrar, M. F. Stuntz. The inexpensive "chart" was a simple color wheel printed on a single sheet of paper. Codes were adapted to suit AHS purposes. Mr. Stuntz recommended that hybridizers consult *A Dictionary of Color* by Maerz and Paul, or the *Royal Horticultural Colour Chart* by Robert F. Wilson, when a more accurate definition was required. The registrar then translated these for the *Check List* according to codes derived from the Fischer Color Chart. (Mr. Stuntz's personal copies of these charts,

the dictionary, and other of his historic documents are on file in the AHS Archives in the Andersen Horticultural Library at Chanhassen, Minnesota.)

In the mid-1950s a concerted effort was made to standardize with an official color chart. George Lenington tells the story:

> Shortly after I became president of this society in 1948, one of the first problems that seemed to need immediate attention was the one concerning the selection of a color chart. Mr. M. Frederick Stuntz was most emphatic in arguing that we put our stamp of approval on the Maerz & Paul Color Dictionary,* yet nearly all the hybridizers that I contacted favored

---

*In a humorous article by Willard King, the author cites as one of the commandments to a top-flight Regional Vice President: Never get into an argument with Fred Stuntz about the Maerz & Paul color chart being inferior to other color charts.

other charts and I even found one of them that used three different charts!

The more I got into the problem, the more complex and confusing it became, so I appointed a color chart committee. Its members were Stanley E. Saxton, chairman, Grafton Shults, and Professor J.B.S. Norton; and I wish to say that no committee will every carry out an assignment more thoroughly or completely, I am sure. Soon I began to receive copies of letters written to various noted color experts, leading flower society officers, organizations such as the Inter-Society Color Council—in fact, anyone and everyone who could furnish any information on the pros and cons of color charts.

After several months of outstanding work by this committee—especially on the part of Grafton Shults—I was given two large three-ring binders filled with pamphlets, color charts, all correspondence and, finally, a four-page summary report by the committee. This report—together with all the material contained in the binders—will prove to be of great value to future color chart committees. After stating the objectives of the committee, the report gave an analysis of various color charts, followed by the summary and recommendation which I give you now:

(Report by Stanley Saxton, June 1949)
. . . Study seems to indicate that at present there is no satisfactory color chart for the color descriptions of daylilies.

Since almost every horticulturist, including the daylily breeders, has already determined his preference and adopted what seems to him a satisfactory chart, there appears no good reason to recommend one specific chart for the use of The Hemerocallis Society, especially since there is no ideal chart for this use.

Until such time as the U.S. Bureau of Standards produces a universal color standard for horticultural use, or until The Hemerocallis Society feels financially able to produce its own chart, it would seem best to use the presently available charts insofar as they solve the problem of color descriptions.

It should also be borne in mind that the same daylily clone will not show the same color tone in two different locations, and that even in the same location, soil, temperature, moisture and growing conditions will greatly alter daylily colors. Perhaps a general description serves its purpose as well as an exact reference to a certain color tab on an elaborate color chart.

The two best charts now available are the Royal Horticultural Chart which covers the more useful color tones and the Color Dictionary which is the better reference for color names.

The committee regrets that it cannot make a direct recommendation of a single chart for all-round use, but since no chart seems entirely practical for our purpose, no advantage would be gained by trying to establish one chart at the expense of another. Rather, an open mind regarding future developments and a readiness to adopt a better system when it appears, seems the better objective.

—STANLEY E. SAXTON
Chairman, Color Chart Committee

Mr. Lenington continues:
To the best of my knowledge, little progress has been made toward an improved color chart. However, considering the recent improvements that have been made in plastics, it could well be that we could now formulate our own color chart at much less cost than seemed the case in 1949. I recommend that a second Color Chart Committee be appointed, in the near future, to continue the work so admirably begun by the first committee.

—GEORGE LENINGTON
(From 1956 Hem. J., Vol. 10, No. 1)

The next committee consisted of Mrs. A.W. Simpson, chairman, Ralph Wheeler, and John Armistead. In May 1958, following its recommendations, the board adopted the Nickerson Color Fan, distributed by the American Horticultural Council, as its official color chart. The simple fan had the advantage of being affordable. A supply was obtained by the Society and sold to the membership at cost ($4.00 per fan). However, the new color fan lived not much longer than some ill-fated $100 daylily fans, and with little "fanfare" the official color chart was dropped. Some of the members said good riddance.

I am pleased to note that the directors of the American Hemerocallis Society have discontinued the sale of the Nickerson Color Fan. I tried to use mine last year but found it very lacking in true matching colors for the *Hemerocallis*. It is not nearly as good as the Wilson Horticultural Chart.

—ELIZABETH NESMITH

The subject lay dormant for several years until the late 1970s when Ned Irish, then serving as chairman of the Scientific Committee, presented a proposal to the board calling for a custom standard color chart. It would be produced specifically for AHS purposes. Much to the disappointment of Mr. Irish, the proposal was dropped for lack of board support.

The most recent interest in a color chart has been generated by Gus Guzinski, member of the Scientific Studies Committee, who favors use of a color chart for purposes of registration. His plan, to include other registration data recommendations, has yet to be unveiled.

The time may come when AHS wishes to consider again adopting a color chart for Check List and other descriptive uses. The concept has much in its favor. Perhaps it would be well for future committees to study these previous attempts before setting out to re-invent the color wheel.

William E. Monroe's Story

(June 11, 1990)

HILE ATTENDING the Valdosta Convention, I was contacted about the appointment as registrar for the Society. Being full of youth and enthusiasm, I expressed my willingness to take on the job. At the fall meeting of the board of directors, I was elected as registrar, effective January 1, 1955.

Without benefit of training, supplies, or equipment, the task was attempted in January, 1955. Since none of the records or files were at my disposal, I had to write the former registrar each time a registration came in to see if the selected name was available. Each registration took at least a month to complete. It was a real relief to me when the records and file of registrations were finally turned over to me late in 1955.

My first group of applications for registration were from Henry Sass in Omaha, Nebraska. The daylilies were BUTTERSCOTCH LANE, BUTTERSCOTCH, CAPITOL DOME, and CANDY. These were on display at the 1956 National Convention in Omaha.

Completing a registration was a slow process for me in 1955. The only piece of equipment was an old Sears portable typewriter and a newly purchased composition book to keep the records of the cash receipts. After receiving word from the former registrar that a name was available, a letter of confirmation was sent to the hybridizer. The Registration Data Sheets were kept in alphabetical order in a three-hole notebook that was a holdover from my college days. At the end of the year, the data sheets were bound in a volume—one for each year. A complete file of the data sheets received from January 1, 1955, to the present is on file here. The data sheets for 1953 and 1954 were sent to me late in 1955. These were put in alphabetical order and bound. They are also here.*

Near the end of the year in 1955, I learned that I had to prepare Check List File Cards (information for the Check Lists) in duplicate for each registration. Finally the end of the year came and I knew five copies of the manuscript had to be prepared for the Registration Report for the AHS editor and members of the Registration Committee. This was a quite a challenge since the deadline for registrations was December 31 and I had made a promise to get the manuscript to the editor by January 3. To meet this deadline, the preparation of the manuscript started the day after Christmas and registrations received after that date were attached separately. Correcting mistakes on five copies of onionskin paper was a real job. The practice of making five copies in this manner stayed in effect until Jim Cooper was president and he recommended that the board authorize five copies to be made on a Xerox® machine. After this

---

* The data sheets have been placed in the AHS Archives in Minnesota since Mr. Monroe's death in 1994.

expense was authorized, the Christmas job was much easier for me. In 1966 the board of directors voted to set the deadline back to December 23 or 24, depending on the last mail delivery before Christmas. This also was a big help, for it meant that no longer did I have to attach those little additions to the report. However, it did mean I was always busy at Christmas time.

The Sears® portable typewriter was used until 1957 when the Society finally had enough money to buy me a secondhand, fifty-dollar, upright Underwood®. This was one of the trade-ins of the Agricultural Extension Service where I was employed, but it did the job until 1969 when Bertie Ferris convinced the board that I should have an electric typewriter. This was highly appreciated, though changing from a manual to an electric was an experience. What a mess I made at first!

Making duplicate copies of the Check List File Cards continued until my retirement from the Agricultural Extension Service at the end of 1976. We had used the so-called NCR (No Carbon Required) in my office. I decided to develop a 3 x 5-inch NCR form with two copies to replace the duplicates. The third copy was sent to the hybridizer when a registration was confirmed. The board agreed to this extra expense. This further reduced the work, but all the time new things were being added.

Among the new things that have been added to registration data are the size of the flower in inches, the ploidy, the form—whether single or double, a listing of registrations by hybridizers, and a list of the current-year introductions. All of these additions take

6-2. *W. E. Monroe, AHS Registrar for 32 years. In this photo, taken near the beginning of his term, he is actually younger than his son as pictured on page 115 in a recent photo.*

time, but the advent of the computer helped out once it was purchased and put into use.

The computer is another story—good, but it has been expensive to the registrar. At a summer meeting of the board of directors, I took along my son

---

CODE NAMES

As a part of the registration process, every hybridizer is assigned a code name or abbreviation for identification purposes. Typically, it consists of the surname of the registrant; however, one or more initials may be added to avoid duplication. The registration code name placed in parenthesis following the cultivar name is widely used in Society literature to credit hybridizers for their work.

Occasionally the initials are confusing. Back in the Age of Darkness, women were encouraged to use their husbands' names in registration. Thus, Mary Doe registered her daylilies under the name Mrs. John Doe. If she was unlucky enough to have a husband who preceded her into the Check List, the abbreviation *Doe* was already taken and she became *Doe, J.* forevermore.

The practice of registering under a social name is no longer encouraged, but the Check Lists are filled with such examples. Like a Social Security number, code names must have permanency if they are to have any value in identification.

[the current registrar, W. C. Monroe] to help convince the board that a computer would be good for the Society. They listened to him and authorized a $5,000 expenditure for a computer. That was something else for a seventy-year-old man to learn—it is hard to teach an old dog new tricks. I spent most of the next year and a half entering the past registrations into the computer. We entered only the name, year of registration, and hybridizer for each cultivar. This data was to be used in the Check Word Program that my son designed to determine if a name is available or not. Entering data for thirty thousand names may not seem like such a chore to a skilled typist, but as you probably know, a computer does not tolerate mistakes. Proofreading the material was more work than entering it in the computer. We did not get the program completely computerized until January 1, 1984.

It was hoped that proofreading the material would eliminate all errors, but it did not. Since 1984, two names have been duplicated, caused not by the computer but by the operator and the proofreader. Both of these errors have been corrected and apologies sent to the hybridizers concerned.

6-3. In 1957, the Registrar received an equipment upgrade.

The Check Word Program in the computer has really saved time in looking up the availability of names. Before the computer it was necessary to check a file of over thirty thousand cards for each name involved. Now it takes less than six seconds once the computer has been "booted up." Also, preparing the manuscript at the end of the year is now a breeze compared to the days when it had to be prepared with the typewriter.

The computer industry was not a stable one in 1983 and many of the companies that sold seemingly good computers then are no longer in business. Because my son had selected the computer and the company that no longer exists, an IBM computer with a larger capacity was purchased with personal funds when the old computer went haywire and parts no longer were available. Since that time, a Hewlett Packard LaserJet® printer has been purchased for the registrar's use, also with personal funds. The old printer is still functional, but it is very slow and noisy.

William E. Monroe continues his recollections:

THE COMBINED CHECK LISTS

The preparation of the first *Cumulative Check List* [the "Brown Check List" printed in 1957] has an interesting history. It has a lot of errors and is far from perfection, but that can be explained to a degree. Neither the manager of the printing office nor the typesetter had ever seen such semi-coded material as used in registrations, especially those registered prior to 1953. I am not sure if the *Check List* is what caused it or not, but the manager had a nervous breakdown during the printing and he is still handicapped. The typesetter committed suicide. So, a few pages being upside-down and other mistakes can be overlooked.

The combined *Check Lists* 1957–1973 [Yellow] and 1973–1983 [Green] are much better publications. They were prepared by AHS editors Ben Parry and John Allgood, each in a different location with a different printer.

In 1989 Registrations broke new ground with the first combined *Check List* to be generated directly from the registrar's data entries, via computer diskette. No longer was outside typesetting required. The electronic transfer, formatting, and editing were accomplished by Ken Cobb on a volunteer basis. [Editor's note: So satisfactory was this method that it continues today for both annual and combined *Check Lists*. The *Journal* editor now prepares the print-ready copy.]

MONETARY MATTERS

William E. Monroe always favored keeping the registration fee as low as possible so as to encourage hybridizers to honor the registration process. Because his "salary" was a percentage of the registration fee, his philosophy resulted in a very low rate of pay. Still, when a fee hike was proposed in 1980 to cover increased postage and printing costs, he managed to delay the inevitable for five years by reducing his percentage by half.

In his final statement to follow, Bill Monroe reveals something of the character and pride that moved him to an unparalleled record of service.

. . . Although the work described above was performed at a very low rate of compensation—never as high as the minimum wage—it has been compensated by two very high honors: the Helen Field Fischer Medal and the Regional Service Award.

The year 1987 ended an official 32 years of service in the office of the AHS Registrar.

—WILLIAM E. MONROE,
AHS Registrar, 1955–1987

A Torch Is Passed

THE READER WILL DETECT a subtle change from singular to plural in the telling of the story above. W. E. Monroe's son became an active participant in the gentle prodding to move his father in the direction of computers. It was a field so foreign to the patriarch of registrations that it required his son to assume the role of morale booster as well as the more practical one of a custom computer programmer.

Convincing his father was half the battle for the younger Bill. As told in the account by his father, W. C. Monroe made an appearance before the board and made an excellent case for computerizing the registration records. By way of personal anecdote, he recalled that his Christmases past had been dominated by his father's need to get the registrations completed before December 31. Although his father's story bears no overtones of martyrdom, it is pretty clear that he did not spend Decembers waiting for Santa Claus. The computer, it was hoped, would relieve some of this pressure.

When William E. Monroe retired as registrar, his son was voted to succeed him. The father/son teamwork had several obvious advantages. However, it did pose a problem of address. Now there were two "Bill Monroes." Yes, the middle initial was different, but the board of directors had difficulty in remembering who belonged to which until Dorothea Boldt provided a clue of association. "Bill E." would stand for *elder*, she said, while "Bill C." stood for *child*. The problem was solved. It is doubtful whether anyone outside the family knows what either initial really stands for.

Although Bill E. Monroe surrendered the title in 1987, he continued to assist his son until serious illness forced him to relinquish the reins. His interest

6-4. W. C. Monroe, AHS Registrar since 1988. (photo 1995)

in registrations did not die until he was laid to rest in February 1994.

As AHS approaches its 50th birthday, William C. Monroe serves the position of AHS registrar. Whether his term will be as long as his father's remains to be seen. It has a different style and exploits his talents in the field of computer technology. Already, this influence has been felt on the Check Lists. It becomes essential to a file hobbled by 38,000 main entries (expected total accumulated registrations by the end of 1995). The streamlining of data processing has only just begun. In no area of the Society does its influence strike a more powerful posture. The question is: If, when, where, and how?

From Day Lily to Daylily (and Day-lily)

Each of the above spellings can be found in modern publications. Which one is correct? Every *Hemerocallis* lover quickly learns that Daylily is the preferred spelling today. Originally, though, Day Lily was the usual form.

When first published in 1923, *Standardized Plant Names* established the preferred spelling as "Daylily." This book reported recommendations of the American Joint Committee on Horticultural Nomenclature, which was created to solve problems caused by lack of uniformity in the names of cultivated plants. In its compiled lists, the committee found "no less than thirty-one genera in which the common name 'Lily,' usually with a qualifying adjective, has been heretofore applied—genera other than the true Lily genus, *Lilium*. In these cases the name 'Lily' has obviously been used on account of the resemblance of the subjects to the true Lily." One of the Committee's goals was to decide on a single preferred common name for each species. Preferably, this common name would be unique and would not contain a name "belonging more properly, according to accepted usage, to some other genus, species, or variety." But a difficulty existed: "Many of these Lily combinations are too well fixed in common usage to change. To overcome this difficulty the Committee has therefore *applied its rules of consolidating these compounds* where a different suitable common name could not be supplied. Examples: Amazonlily (Eucharis), *not* Amazon Lily; Daylily (Hemerocallis), *not* Day Lily; Glorylily (Gloriosa). . . . No other satisfactory solution of this major difficulty was discovered, and this procedure is believed to be sound." [Above quotes from *Standardized Plant Names*, 1923 edition, Preface, page x]

These consolidated spellings gained immediate acceptance among horticulturists in most cases, and so "Daylily" is found in virtually every horticultural publication since. A few use Day-lily. The nomenclature committee later stated that it "prefers and prints Daylily. It makes no serious objection to Day-lily. It objects very positively to Day Lily, which is apt to mean, for anyone not familiar with the plant, that it is a species or variety of the genus *Lilium*." [Quoted from *Standardized Plant Names*, 1942 edition, Preface, page vii, footnote, example changed from Mayapple to Daylily]

Unfortunately, *Webster's Dictionary* and many other "standard" references such as encyclopedias have not yet adopted the preferred spelling, so "Day Lily" still shows up in newspaper articles and so on. Maybe they will catch up in the second fifty years.

Patricia Crooks Henley
4-20-95

Chapter 7

Discovery

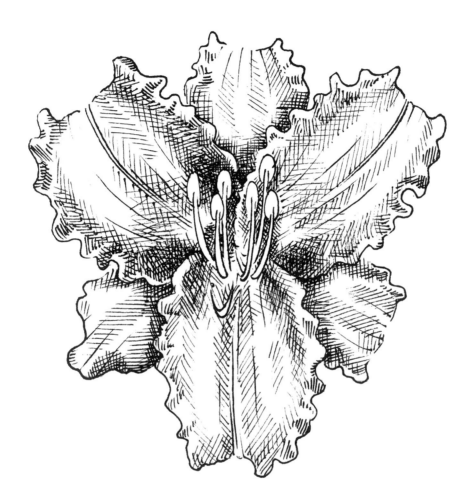

*Aristotle could have avoided the mistake of thinking
that women have fewer teeth than men by the simple
device of asking Mrs. Aristotle to open her mouth.*
BERTRAND RUSSELL

Scientists We Have Known

HE TITANS OF YESTERYEAR were a busy lot. To follow A.B. Stout around, even through the pages of his book, is to experience a degree of tenacity not often found in today's society of attention-deficit disorders. Yes, our early scientists were a hard act to follow. Rocking-chair critics may see the golden age of science as being in the past tense; but, to be fair, the playing field has changed:

• *The wellspring of government largesse has dried up.* Fewer grants are available for specialized studies.
• *Those early-bird scientists got there first.* New researchers are finding that few virgin fields remain to be explored.
• *The composition of the Society has changed.* A lower percentage of members are inclined toward science.

In reality, the daylily's development has occurred in step-like progression, spanning the 20th century—

George Yeld produced the first known *Hemerocallis* hybrid in England in 1893.

Amos Perry followed suit with several hybrids that found their way into America.

Arlow Burdette Stout produced his first paper on daylilies for the New York Botanical Gardens in 1919.

The American Amaryllis Society (later to become the American Plant Life Society) was formed in Florida in the 1930s. Because of the close relationship of the daylily to the amaryllis, this society devoted considerable research and publication space to *Hemerocallis*.

All of this activity took place before AHS came into existence.

The editor of the American Plant Life Society's excellent *Herbertia* was one Hamilton P. Traub, a distinguished plant scientist who attracted writers and members of his own kind. Furthermore, Dr. Traub's career moves had the effect of distributing his infectious enthusiasm from Florida to Maryland and finally to California. Through it all, he maintained his editorship of *Herbertia*. When AHS was formed, Dr. Traub joined and became a vital component of the Society's scientific pool.

University sponsorships and the backing of the United States Department of Agriculture accounted for much of the scientific work that was done with daylilies in the 1960s and 1970s. Before the public began to cry "pork barrel," grants for the study of highly specialized subjects—critics might say *obscure* subjects—were relatively easy to come by.

In the 1952 *Yearbook*, Thomas Manley reports on the effect of specific mulches on daylilies as observed in Valleevue Test Gardens of Western Reserve University in Ohio.

Projects were undertaken at the University of Chicago by Ezra Kraus, Paul Voth, and Robert A. Griesbach. This respected institution was a "feeding station" for the Chicago Area Hybridizers. The charismatic Dr. Kraus later served at Oregon State where he continued to interest himself and others in research with daylilies.

At one time the United States Department of Agriculture in Beltsville, Maryland, had studies underway for many specific ornamentals. One was *Hemerocallis*. Dr. Traub, George Darrow, Robert A. Griesbach, and Toru Arisumi are among the AHS member/scientists who did research at the USDA. In exchange for furnishing the agency with booklets for distribution, AHS received permission to publish important scientific papers dealing with daylilies. Costs to the Society were negligible since the required booklets were printed from *Journal* plates.

California was another hot spot for research. Quinn Buck, Hamilton Traub, and Robert Schreiner were the first to record pioneer work with colchicine-treated daylilies. All three men eventually worked out of California, although Dr. Traub did his initial conversions at the USDA in Beltsville, Maryland, and Robert Schreiner reported his first successful conversions as a student at the University of Minnesota in 1947. Vernon Stoutmeyer, on the USDA team at Beltsville with Dr. Traub, later took a position at the University of California with his former teacher and Quinn Buck. An interesting article by Mr. Buck appears in the 1951 Yearbook in which he gives a cautious preliminary summary of tetraploid expectations based on his conversions of SOUDAN (Stout) and other early trials: "Colchicine is a useful tool in plant breeding in rather a restricted sense."

The Louisiana Agricultural Experiment Station in Baton Rouge served as an early daylily test garden and issued periodic reports. (This was Registrar Bill E. Monroe's place of regular employment before he retired in 1976.)

The Deep South had a strong interest in finding answers to the worrisome problem of rot, which has a higher incidence in that part of the country. In the 1970s, James A. Spencer, Associate Plant Pathologist at the Mississippi Agricultural and Forestry Experiment Station, directed a study on rot in daylilies and furnished the *Journal* with papers recommending cultural controls. Unfortunately, the subject of the study has not been stamped out.

Also in the 1970s, several studies were undertaken with the object of speeding nature's method of propagation for daylilies. Both Vernon Stoutmeyer at UCLA and Martin J. Meyer, Jr. of the University of Illinois published papers in the *Daylily Journal* relating to tissue culture. Meanwhile, the AHS supported a study that would lead to the use of BAP IAA paste on sheared ramets to encourage vegetative offshoots. This work was carried out under the leadership of Michael Kasha with John Kirby-Smith at Florida State University.

Michael Kasha and two other members of the Florida State team, Katherine Bisset and Pradeep Sengupta, also directed a search for the blue daylily. It was an interesting hypothesis, but it did not translate into the desired results.

The mystique of color has lured both scientists and laymen. Each group claims success in broadening the spectrum. It is an area of stunning payback.

Other subjects that have intrigued scientists are seed germination, pest control, and chromosomes.

Researchers sometimes work in conjunction with the AHS's Scientific Studies program, but a great deal of significant work has come about through the independent efforts of interested members. The advancement of daylilies can use all hands.

FARTHER AFIELD

Currently, the AHS supports the cataloging and collection of *Hemerocallis* species at the United States National Arboretum. This represents a continuing effort on the part of the Society to bring some order into a confusing subject. Field trips have been reported in the *Journal*—the lengthy Shiu-Ying Hu papers on Chinese species, and the Apps-Batdorf report on Korean species. The most recent contribution to the species papers is John Schabell's series, primarily a collection of referenced quotes, that concludes with V. 50, No. 1 of the *Daylily Journal*.

The AHS Scientific Studies Committee occasionally teams with other Society committees in pursuing special projects. A booklet, *Handbook for Daylily Registration*, has been approved and is being prepared by Gus Guzinski, Chairman of the Scientific Research Projects Subcommittee. It will contain scientific definitions, word descriptions, drawings, and other items to aid the registration process, subject to approval of the board and Registration Committee. It is hoped that this work will clarify the long-standing multiple interpretations that have beset flower forms, such as spiders, doubles, and now "polytepals." Perhaps it will even get into the tumultuous color-chart business again.

TETRAPLOID LEADERS

Arguably, the most important contribution made by daylily researchers has been the development of tetraploids. The colchicine method of chromosome doubling was discovered in 1937 and applied to daylilies in 1947, but its impact on the grower and backyard hybridizer did not become apparent until the curtain was drawn back at the Chicago Convention in 1961. There it was greeted with a controversy that reverberated all the way to England. Virginia Peck records the great happening and its aftermath with delightful humor in the Summer 1989 issue of the *Daylily Journal*. Suffice to say, the Montagues and Capulets had nothing on the tet and dip camps that formed after Chicago.

It might be noted that Virginia Peck, whose area of expertise was English literature, plunged into the pool of scientists as neatly as she broke the waters in her championship dives. She took the trouble to educate herself thoroughly in theory and practice. Soon she was out-tetraploiding the great ones from Chicago, Maryland, and California. Some of the Society's most valuable literature on the subject of tetraploids was written by Virginia Peck.

FUNDING RESEARCH

As attrition reduces the number of dedicated scientists faster than they can be replaced, AHS faces the problem of funding new research. Thanks to the Joe House Memorial Fund, established to honor one of the Society's former presidents, science has better financial backing than most committees of the AHS. Even so, it cannot touch the enormous cost of outside research today. The Society attempts to select worthy projects to subsidize in a modest way. It cannot afford to pick up the whole tab.

DIFFERENT STROKES

At the outset of this chapter it was noted that the character of the Society has changed. The very diversity of the membership that makes it interesting also makes it challenging. There will always be members who prefer a de-emphasis on scientific material. In 1960, one such correspondent pleaded with the editor for the return of "warmth and homeyness" to the *Yearbooks*: ". . . all this has been replaced by technical and rather dull (to the amateur grower) articles on hybridizing and exchange of comments by commercial growers." She concedes that "some articles of this sort are helpful and necessary, but not to the exclusion of subjects of more general interest." (At that time, each volume had a *Yearbook* which generally concentrated the disputed technical information in one place and left three pamphlet-sized *Journals* for those who preferred the user-friendly approach.)

The letter prompted a rebuttal in the next *Journal* from Virginia Peck, "In Defense of Science." In this she states, "We owe to the scientists and their writings, ultimately, the fact that we have the Society publications at all, and even the Society itself." She points out the difficulty of haunting libraries, sifting through highly technical professional scientific journals, just to acquire the requisite knowledge for effective hybridizing. She concludes firmly, "It seems to me that the logical place for a *Hemerocallis* grower to find out what he needs to know about *Hemerocallis* is in the publications of the American Hemerocallis Society."

On balance, the Society may find a reduced ratio of members on the side of science; nonetheless, readers of every persuasion must bear in mind that scientific studies are for the benefit of all.

Science In Print

 LONG-STANDING AMBITION of this editor has been to make available a complete bibliography of scientific material published by the Society. It did not happen for this book. In fact, a major hurdle is identification of scientific material as such. Articles fall into broad categories of popular science, pseudo-science, and pure science. To make the distinction, a scientist should be involved. Some *Journal* editors have been scientists—to the great benefit of their publications—but that happy circumstance does not include present company.

Operating under the assumption that half a loaf is better than none, we are presenting two separate lists which, unfortunately, do not combine to make a whole. On the other hand, both lists extend beyond the literature of the Society, so perhaps they exceed the ambition of this editor. Both deal with daylilies but each is somewhat specialized. The first was compiled by Virginia Peck for inclusion in the *Check List* supplement, 1960 *Hemerocallis Clones* (the accepted terminology of the day).

The second bibliography was a joint effort of the Science/Species Robin and the AHS Scientific Studies Committee under the direction of James R. Brennan.

Some deletions have been made to avoid duplication between lists.

A BIBLIOGRAPHY OF THE LITERATURE
ON GENETICS AND BREEDING OF HEMEROCALLIS
by Virginia Peck

Baker, Ruth E. "Seedling Bed." *American Hemerocallis Society 1955 Yearbook*, p. 76.

Ballard, R. W. "Wanted: Daylily Inheritance Data." *Herbertia*, X (January 1954), 59-61.

Ballard, W. D. "Daylily Notes, 1954." *Herbertia*, XI (January 1955), 79-80.

Ballard, W. R. "Daylily Breeding Project." *Herbertia*, IX (January 1953), 89-90.

Ballard, W. R. "Progress in Daylily Breeding." *Plant Life*, VIII (January-October, 1952), 96-97.

Ballard, W. R. "Why Neglect the Night-Bloomers?" *Herbertia*, XIV (1947), 137 138.

Barnett Mrs. E. Clyde. "More About the Clone Garnet Robe." *The Hemerocallis Journal*, XIV (January-March, 1960), 22.

Bechtold, Le Moine. "Hemerocallis, 1922-1956." *The Hemerocallis Journal and Yearbook*, 1956, p. 53.

Benzinger, Fred M. "Response of Certain Hemerocallis Clones to Supplementary Light Treatment." *The Hemerocallis Journal* XIV (January-March 1960), 18-19.

Buch, Philip O. "First–Daylilies, Then–Nightlilies, Now–Tudaylilies!" *The Hemerocallis Society 1954 Yearbook*. pp. 24-26.

Buck, W. Quinn. "Colchicine As a Tool in Breeding." *The Hemerocallis Society 1950 Yearbook*, pp. 33-34.

Buck, W. Quinn. "Colchicine-induced Polyploidy in Daylilies (Hemerocallis)." *Journal of California Horticultural Society*, X (October, 1949), 161.

Buck, W. Quinn. "Looking at Tetraploid Daylilies." *American Hemerocallis Society 1955 Yearbook*, pp. 86-87.

Buck, W. Quinn. "Pollen Longevity and Storage." *The Hemerocallis Society 1952 Yearbook*, p. 50.

Buck, W. Quinn. "Results with Colchicine." *The Hemerocallis Society 1952 Yearbook*, p. 74.

Burge, Joan S. "Seven Years with Milliken Daylilies." *The Hemerocallis Society Yearbook 1953*, pp. 98-101.

Burtner R. H. "Some Hybridizing Experiences." *The Hemerocallis Society 1950 Yearbook*, pp. 69-70.

Buss, Walter. "Where Do We Go From Here?" *The Hemerocallis Society 1950 Yearbook*, pp. 63-67.

Chandler, Clyde. "Microsporogenesis in Triploid and Diploid Plants of *Hemerocallis fulva*." *Bulletin of the Torrey Botanical Club*, LXVII (1940), 649-672.

Christ, John C. "Some Genetic Principles Involved in Hybridizing Hemerocallis." *Midwest Hemerocallis Society 1948 Yearbook*, pp. 24-26.

Cooley, J. S. "Economy in Growing Daylily Seedlings." *Herbertia*, XIV (1947), 142-143.

Corliss, Philip G. "Genetics: Inherited Hem Characteristics." *The Hemerocallis Journal and Yearbook*, 1958, pp. 109-113.

Corliss, Philip G. "Genetics: Inherited Hem Characteristics." *The Hemerocallis Journal and Yearbook*, 1959, pp. 88-93.

Corliss, Philip G. "Let's Go Shopping for Daylilies." *American Home*. LI (May, 1954), 60-61.

Corliss, Philip G. "Multiple Scapes on Hemerocallis." *Herbertia*, XI (January, 1955), 75-77.

Corliss, Philip G. "New Pink Daylilies." *Flower Grower*, XXXVIII (July, 1951), 21.

Corliss, Philip G. "Where Do the Hybridizers Go From Here?" *The Hemerocallis Journal*, X (July-September, 1956), 18-19, 22.

Corliss, Philip G. "Hybridizing for Late-Bloomers." *The Hemerocallis Society 1950 Yearbook*. pp. 71-72.

Corliss, Philip G. "Why I Hybridize." *The First Yearbook of the Midwest Hemerocallis Society*, (March, 1947), p. 55.

Couglin, Orville C. "Hemerocallis Breeding and the Prospects Ahead." *Midwest Hemerocallis Society 1948 Yearbook*. pp. 32-33.

Davis, B. A. "Build Your Garden Around Daylilies." *Flower Grower*, XLII (June 1955), 48.

Davis, B. A. "Daylilies and How to Grow Them." *Flower Grower*, XLI (July 1954), 36-37.

Davis, B. A. "Daylilies Have a Long Pedigree." *Flower Grower*, XLIV (July, 1957), 40-41.

Davis, Claude W. " For Southern Gardeners." *The Hemerocallis Journal and Yearbook*, 1958, pp. 136-137.

Douglas, Geddes. "Color Change Explained." *The Hemerocallis Society 1953 Yearbook*, pp. 47-48.

Douglas, Geddes. "Modern American Daylilies." *Royal Horticultural Society Journal*, LXXVIII (May, 1953), 171-177.

Ellison, W. J. "Modern Daylily." *Your Garden and Home*, II (June, 1948), 20+.

Emigholz, Florence. "Why We Hybridize." *The First Yearbook of the Midwest Hemerocallis Society* (March, 1947), p. 54.

Ferrick, Daisy L. "Daylilies in the Pink." *Flower and Garden*, III (July, 1959), 28-29.

Ferrick, Daisy L. "General Aims in Hybridizing." *The First Yearbook of the Midwest Hemerocallis Society* (March, 1947), p. 53.

Fischer, Hubert A. "Over Fifteen Years With Kraus Daylilies." *The Hemerocallis Journal*, XI (January–March, 1957), 4-6.

Gerlach, M. E. "Hybridizing Daylilies." *Flower Grower*, XL (June, 1953), 67.

Gilmer, George. "Five Distinctive Hemerocallis." *Amaryllis Yearbook*, XVI (January, 1960), 141-142.

Gilmer, George. "Hemerocallis of the Future." *Herbertia*, XII (January, 1956), 82–84.

Gilmer, George. "New Hemerocallis Hybrids Wanted." *Herbertia*, XV (1948), 81-82.

Goddard, Myra E. "H. M. Russell, Daylily Hybridizer and Grower." *The Hemerocallis Society 1949 Yearbook*, pp. 27-30.

Griesbach, R. A. "Cold Temperature Treatment as a Means of Breaking Seed Dormancy in Hemerocallis." *The Hemerocallis Journal and Yearbook*. 1956, pp. 85-90.

Griesbach, R. A. "Some Aspects of Hemerocallis Seed Germination." *American Hemerocallis Society 1955 Yearbook*, pp. 26-29.

Griesbach, R. A. "Some Notes on the Harvesting and Storing of Daylily Seeds." *The Hemerocallis Journal and Yearbook 1957*, pp. 58-60.

Griesbach, R. A., and Paul D. Voth. "On Seed Dormancy and Seed Germination in Hemerocallis." *The Botanical Gazette*, CXVIII (1957), 223–237.

Hager, Ben R. "The Daylilies of Carl Milliken." *The Hemerocallis Journal and Yearbook*, 1959, pp. 96-102.

Hall, David F. "Hybridizing Hemerocallis." *The Hemerocallis Society 1954 Yearbook*, pp. 7-10.

Hall, David F. "Hybridizing in Arkansas." *The First Yearbook of the Midwest Hemerocallis Society*, (March, 1947), p. 70.

Hava, Walter C. "Necessity—The Mother of Invention." *The Hemerocallis Journal and Yearbook* 1960 pp. 31-33.

Hava, Walter C. "Pollens." *The Hemerocallis Journal and Yearbook*, 1958, pp. 76-78.

Henry, Mary G. "A Sectorial Mutation in Hemerocallis." *Plant Life*, VI (January-October, 1950), 111–112.

Henry, Mary G. "Hemerocallis—Gladwyne Chimera." *Plant Life*, VIII (January October, 1952), 92-94.

Hill, H. M. "Our Hybridizing Goals." *The First Yearbook of the Midwest Hemerocallis Society* (March, 1947), p. 69.

Hindman, Olive M. "Seed Sowing Experiments." *The Hemerocallis Society 1951 Yearbook*, p. 42.

Holmes, A. V. "Exciting Lavender Daylilies." *Flower Grower*, XLV (July, 1958), 34.

Hurst, Lewis A. "Daylily Breeding As a Hobby." *Herbertia*, XIV (1947), 138-139.

"Hybridization and Selective Breeding in the Genus Hemerocallis." *Proceedings of the Seventh International Genetical Congress*. Edinburgh, Scotland (August, 1939), pp. 277-278.

"Hybridizing the Hemerocallis." *Plants and Garden* XV (Summer, 1959), 39.

Johnson, B. Lennart and Austin Griffiths, Jr. "Effect of Temperature and Humidity on the Longevity of Hemerocallis Pollen as Measured by Its Ability to Effect Capsule and Seed Set." *Proceedings of the American Society for Horticultural Science*, LV, 1950.

Johnson, R. "Make Your Own Daylilies." *Flower Grower*, XLV (September, 1958), 67.

Kennell, Everett H. "Observations of a Daylily Hobbyist." *Plant Life*, VI (January-October, 1950), 58-59.

King, Willard A. "Sucker for Daylilies." *The Hemerocallis Society 1953 Yearbook*. pp. 49-51.

Knotts, Bev. "Luscious Lavender Daylilies for Your Garden." *Flower and Garden*, IV (July, 1960), 27+.

Kraus, E. J. "Double Flowered Hemerocallis." *The Hemerocallis Society 1953 Yearbook* pp. 57-60.

Kraus, E. J. "Notes on Hybridizing." *The Hemerocallis Society 1949 Yearbook*, pp. 66-74.

Kraus, E. J. "Some Further Notes on Hybridizing." *The Hemerocallis Journal and Yearbook*, 1956, p. 120.

Leonian, Nell Lanham. "The Leonian Hemerocallis Breeding Stock." *Herbertia*, XIV (1947), 133-134.

Lord, Arthur R. "End of Man in a Hurry." *The Hemerocallis Journal*, XIII (July-September, 1959), 20-21.

Lord, Arthur R. "Man in a Hurry." *The Hemerocallis Journal*, XIII (January–March, 1959), 23-24.

MacArthur, Mrs. W. E. "My Daylily Interest." *Herbertia*, XIV (1947), 161-162.

Miles, James F. "Double Daylilies." *The Hemerocallis Journal and Yearbook*, 1959, pp. 94-96.

Miller, L. E. "Mecca for Daylily Fans; Garden in Bartlesville, Oklahoma." *Flower Grower*, XL (May, 1953), 46 -47.

Munson R. W. "An Approach to Hybridizing." *The Hemerocallis Journal and Yearbook*, 1960, pp. 119-122.

Myers, Everett C. "Needed Research on Hemerocallis." *The Hemerocallis Journal and Yearbook*, 1958, pp. 114-122.

Myers, Everett C. "New Breeding Angles for Day lilies." *The Hemerocallis Journal*, XIII (October-December, 1959), 1-3.

Myers, Everett C. "Sidelights on Albino Daylilies." *The Hemerocallis Journal and Yearbook*, 1957, pp. 54-58.

Nesmith, Elizabeth N. "Adventures in Hybridizing." *The Hemerocallis Society 1954 Yearbook*, pp. 10-11.

Nesmith, Elizabeth N. "My Interest in Hemerocallis." *The First Yearbook of the Midwest Hemerocallis Society*, (March, 1947), pp. 59–61.

Nesmith, Elizabeth N. "New Developments in Daylilies." *Journal of the New York Botanical Garden*, XXXVI (1934), 205-216.

Nesmith, Elizabeth N. "Notes on Hybridizing and Culture." *The Hemerocallis Journal and Yearbook*, 1958, pp. 74-76.

Nesmith, Elizabeth N. "Notes on Hybridizing Hemerocallis." *Plants and Garden*, XL (Summer, 1959), 37-39.

Nesmith, Elizabeth N. "Problems in Hybridizing." *The Hemerocallis Journal and Yearbook*, 1959, pp. 64 -66.

Nesmith, Elizabeth N. "Producing New Varieties." *The Hemerocallis Journal and Yearbook*, 1956, p. 106.

Norton, J. B. "Double Hemerocallis Flower." *The Hemerocallis Society 1950 Yearbook*, pp. 39-40.

Norton, J. B. "Hemerocallis From Seed to Seed." *The Hemerocallis Society 1950 Yearbook*, pp. 41-45.

Norton, J. B. "Making New Daylilies." *Herbertia*, XIV (1947), 134-137.

Otis, Charles H. "On the Occurrence of Mutations." The *Hemerocallis Journal and Yearbook* 1959, pp. 83-88.

Otis, Charles H. "The Results of Crossing Diploid and Triploid Hemerocallis: Preliminary." *The Hemerocallis Journal and Yearbook*, 1960, pp. 104-112.

Peck, Virginia. "Amateur Hybridizing of Daylilies." The *Hemerocallis Journal*, XIII (July-September, 1959), 22-23, 33-34.

Peck, Virginia. "Pollen-tube Behavior in Self-incompatibility." *Report of the Proceedings of the Fifth International Botanical Congress*. Cambridge, England (1930), pp. 255-256.

Price, M. "Red Daylilies Command Attention." *Flower Grower*, XLVI (August, 1959), 32.

Randall, H. J. "Day Lilies." *Royal Horticultural Society Journal*, LXXXIV (January, 1959), 5-10.

Redding, Ruth. "Experiences of an Amateur Pollen Dauber." *The Hemerocallis Journal*, XIV (January-March, 1960), 23-24.

Russell, H. M. "Cinderella Lily Now a Princess." *Nature Magazine* XXXVII (May, 1944), 264-266.

Sass, Hans P. "My Quest for Stars." *Midwest Hemerocallis Society 1948 Yearbook*, pp. 30-31.

Sass, Henry E. "Our Aims in Breeding." *The First Yearbook of the Midwest Hemerocallis Society* (March, 1947), p. 69.

Saxton, Stanley E. "Adventures in Breeding Hemerocallis." *Herbertia*, IX (January, 1953), 86-89.

Saxton, Stanley E. "Adventures in Daylily Growing." *The First Yearbook of the Midwest Hemerocallis Society* (March 1947), p. 71.

Saxton, Stanley E. "Breeding Miniature Daylilies." *Herbertia*, XII (January 1956) 80–82.

Saxton, Stanley E. "Daylilies, Miniature." *Flower Grower*, XXXIX (July, 1952), 29.

Saxton, Stanley E. "Hemerocallis From Seed—For Northern Gardeners." *The Hemerocallis Journal and Yearbook*, 1958, pp. 135-136.

Saxton, Stanley E. "New Developments in Daylilies." *Garden Journal of the New York Botanical Garden*, IX (July 1959), 130-136.

Saxton, Stanley E. "The Wheeler Daylilies." *Midwest Hemerocallis Society 1948 Yearbook*, pp. 44-48.

Schreiner, Robert. "Dabbling with Daylilies." *Midwest Hemerocallis Society 1948 Yearbook*, pp. 40-43.

Seckman, M. C. "Lilies for a Day and a Decade." *Home Garden*, XIV (August 1949), 41-46.

Shaver, Donald L., Mary Price Aubertin, and G. M. Fosler. "Chromosome Numbers in Various Horticultural Clones of Hemerocallis." *The Hemerocallis Journal and Yearbook*, 1958, pp. 105-109.

Shull, J. Marion. "Fascination Daylilies—The Beginning of a Hobby." *Herbertia*, XIV (1947), 129-133.

Shults, Grafton W. "Hemerocallis Breeding—The Hurst Band System." *Plant Life*, V (January-October 1949), 102.

Shults, Grafton W. "Hemerocallis X-Ray Mutation." *The Hemerocallis Journal and Yearbook*, 1959, pp. 81-82.

Stevens, Helen. "A Hyperion Mutation." *The Hemerocallis Society 1952 Yearbook*, pp. 77-78.

Stout, A. B. (See entries listed in Bibliography II)

Stout, A. B. "Chromosome Numbers in *Hemerocallis* With Reference to Triploidy and Secondary Polyploidy." *Cytologia*, III (1932), 250-259.

Stout, A. B. "Daylilies of Today." *Garden Journal of the New York Botanical Garden*, V (January 1955), 10-11.

Stout, A. B. *Daylilies*. The Macmillan Company: New York, 1934.

Stout, A. B. "Daylilies of Today." *Flower Grower*, XXXVIII (July, 1951), 18–19.

Stout, A. B. "Notes on Some New Daylilies." *Flower Grower*, XXXVI (July 1949), 609.

Stout, A. B. "Some Results of Selective Breeding with Hemerocallis." *Records of the Genetic Society of America* (1936).

Stout, A. B. "The Tall Daylilies." *The Hemerocallis Society 1949 Yearbook*, pp. 59-66.

Stout, A. B. "The Theron Daylily." *The First Yearbook of the Midwest Hemerocallis Society* (March 1947), pp. 57–58.

Stout, A. B. "Types of Anthesis in Hemerocallis and Their Heredity in Hybrids." *Bulletin of the Torrey Botanical Club*, LXXIII (1946), 154+. Reprinted in *The Hemerocallis Journal*, XIV (July-September 1960), 10-30.

Stout, A. B. "Variegation and Somatic Mutations in Daylilies." *The Hemerocallis Journal and Yearbook*, 1956, pp. 15-21.

Stout, A. B., and T. Susa. "Chromosome Irregularities in Relation to Sterility in Hemerocallis fulva clone EUROPA." *Annals of the New York Academy of Science*, XXXI (1929), 1-30.

Stout, A. B., and C. Chandler. "Pollen-tube Behavior in Hemerocallis with Special Reference to Incompatibilities." *Bulletin of the Torrey Botanical Club*, LX (1933), 397-416.

Stout, A. B., and C. Chandler. "Studies of the Inheritance of Self and Cross-Incompatibility." *Memoirs of the Horticultural Society of New York*, III (1927), 345-352.

Tanahashi, Takashi. "Hybridizing in the Rain." *The Hemerocallis Society 1949 Yearbook*, pp. 74-75.

Taylor, Mrs. Bright. "My Work as a Hybridist." *The First Yearbook of the Midwest Hemerocallis Society* (March, 1947), p. 68.

Tiemann, Olga R. "How Do Your Hemerocallis Measure Up?" *Flower and Garden*, IV (June 1960) 34-35.

Traub, Hamilton P. "A Convenient Desiccator for Storing Pollen." *Herbertia*, III (1936), 104-106.

Traub, Hamilton P. "Colchicine-Induced *Hemerocallis* Polyploids and Their Breeding Behavior." *Plant Life*, VII (1951), 83–116.

Traub, Hamilton P. "Colchicine Poisoning in Relation to *Hemerocallis* and Some Other Plants." *Science*, CX (1949), 686–687.

Traub, Hamilton P. "Daylily Breeding in Subtropical Florida." *Herbertia*, VII (1940), 151-157. Reprinted in *The First Yearbook of the Midwest Hemerocallis Society* (March 1947), pp. 62-64.

Traub, Hamilton P. "First Decade of *Hemerocallis Washingtonia*." *Herbertia*, XV (January, 1959), 69-79. Reprinted in *The Hemerocallis Journal and Yearbook*, 1960, pp. 65-75. Part II *The Hemerocallis Journal and Yearbook*, 1963 pp. 77-86.

Traub, Hamilton P. "First Decade of *Hemerocallis Washingtonia*." *Amaryllis Yearbook*, XVI (January 1960), 111-120.

Traub, Hamilton P. "Hemerocallis Clone Mayor Starzynski?" *Herbertia*, VI (1939), 156.

Traub, Hamilton P. "The 'Wyndham Hayward' Tetraploid Daylily." *Herbertia*, XV (January 1959), 31.

Traub, Hamilton P. "Triploid Daylilies." *Euclides*, XIV (1959), 221.

Voth, Paul D. "Self-Fertility of Daylilies Derived from Clones 'Dolly Varden,' 'Dominion.'" *American Hemerocallis Society 1955 Yearbook*, pp. 66-70.

Watkins, John V. "Dwarf Daylilies." *The Hemerocallis Journal and Yearbook*, 1956, pp. 131-132.

Watkins, John V. "Helpful Suggestions for Amateur Daylily Hybridizers." *The Hemerocallis Society 1950 Yearbook*, pp. 33–37.

Watkins, John V. "New Daylily Developments." *Horticulture*, XXVII (June 1949), 221.

Watkins, John V. "Selective Hemerocallis Breeding at the University of Florida." *Herbertia*, XIV (1947), 141-142.

Watkins, John V. "Variegated Daylilies in Florida." *The Hemerocallis Journal and Yearbook*, 1957, p. 53.

Wheeler, Ralph W. "New Daylilies From Old." *Herbertia*, XIV (1947), 10-18.

Woodroffe, F. B. "Great Daylilies Ahead." *House and Garden*, LXXVII (April 1940), 42.

BIBLIOGRAPHY II

Acknowledgments

The following bibliography was compiled under the direction of Scientific Studies Chairman Jim Brennan, with the assistance of the 1994-1995 Scientific Studies committee and the Science/Species Round Robin. Much credit is due to Carl Sigel for use of his species-oriented bibliography as a starting point. The list has been expanded to include diversified subjects, and while entries are not all technical, researchers may find subject-related material of interest. This list is intended to update, expand, and complement the 1960 Peck bibliography.

Apps, D. A. and Batdorf, L. 1988. The Search for, and the Evaluation of Korean Daylily Species. Daylily Jour. 43: 11-19.

Apps, D. A. and Heuser, C. W. 1975. Vegetative propagation of *Hemerocallis* - including tissue culture. Proc. Plt. Prop. Soc. 25: 362-67.

Araki, Y. 1952. *Hemerocallis sempervirens*. Jour. Jap. Bot. 27: 255-56.

Arisumi, T. 1966. Colchicine-Induced Tetraploid and Cytochimeral Daylilies. Hem. Jour. Yearbook 1966 pp. 59-67.

Arisumi, T. 1963. Effects of Chilling and Daylength on Growth and Flowering of Daylilies. Proc. Amer. Soc. Hort. Sci. 83: 798-802.

Arisumi, T. 1962. Effects of Forcing Temperatures on the Growth, Flowering, and Seed Set of *Hemerocallis* cv. Purity. Proc. Amer. Soc. Hort. Sci. 81: 518-20.

Arisumi, T. 1965. Screening Diploid and Tetraploid Progenies of Daylilies by Stomal Size. Proc. Amer. Soc. Hort. Sci. 87: 479-85. (Also Hem. Jour. 28: #2 pp. 38-44.

Arisumi, T. 1970. Experiments in Breeding for Triploid Daylilies. Hem. Jour. 24: 33-37.

Arisumi, T. 1970. Effect of Temperature During Pollination and Fertilization on Seed Set in *Hemerocallis*. Hem. Jour. 24: 28-32.

Arisumi, T. 1970. Inheritance of Red Flower Color in *Hemerocallis*. Hem. Jour. 24: #4 9-14.

Arisumi, T. 1972. Stabilities of Colchicine-Induced Tetraploid and Cytochimeral Daylilies. Hem. Jour. 26: #4 pp. 25-31. (see correction: Hem. Jour. 27: #1 p.17.

Arisumi, T. 1971. The Changing *Hemerocallis*. Hem. Jour. 25: 10-16.

Arisumi, T. 1971. Cytology and Chromosome Numbers of Modern *Hemerocallis*. Hem. Jour. 25: #2 pp. 30-37.

Arisumi, T. 1971. Triploidy as a Cause of Low Fertility in "Garnet Robe." Hem. Jour. 25: #1 32-37.

Arisumi, T. & Frazier, L. C. 1968. The Initial and Early Developmental Stages of the Floral Scape in *Hemerocallis*. Proc. Amer. Soc. Hort. Sci. 93: 604-609. (Also Hem. Jour. 28: #3 17-22.)

Asen, S. and Arisumi, T. 1968. Anthocyanins from *Hemerocallis*. Proc. Amer. Soc. Hort. Sci. 92: 641-645.

Bailey, L. 1930. *Hemerocallis*: the Daylilies. Gentes Herberum 2: 143-156.

Bailey, L. H. 1933. *Hemerocallis*. The Standard 2: 1455-1457.

Baker, G. P. 1937. *Hemerocallis*: the Day Lily. Jour. Royal Hort. Soc. 62: 399-411.

Barr, T. C. and Munson, R. W. 1985. The Evolution of Red Tetraploid *Hemerocallis*. Daylily Jour. 39: 316-323, 370-378.

Barr, T. C. 1987. *Hemerocallis* and the New Plant Biosystematics. Daylily Jour. 42: 36-39.

Baum, L.C. 1973. (Reprint Reg. 13 N.L.) What is a Tetraploid? Hem. Jour. 27: #1 pp.17-20.

Belling, J. 1921. Chromosomes of *Canna* and of *Hemerocallis*. Proc. Nat. Acad. Sci. 7: 197-201.

Belling, J. 1925. Chromosomes of *Canna* and of *Hemerocallis*. Jour. Hered. 16: 465-466.

Benzinger, F. M. 1968. Propagation of Daylilies. Amer. Hort. Mag. 47: 194-196

Benzinger, F. M. 1977. Should We Convert Diploids to Tetraploids? Hem. Jour. 31: #2 pp. 23-27.

Bielski, R. L. 1993. Fructan Hydrolysis Drives Petal Expansion in the Ephemeral Daylily Flower. Plt. Phys. 103: 213-219.

Bielski, R. L. and Reid, M. S. 1992. Physiological Changes Accompanying Senescence in the Ephemeral Daylily Flower. Plt. Phys. 98: 1042-1049.

Bisset, K. E. 1976. Spectrophotometry, Chromatography, and Genetics of *Hemerocallis* Pigments. Florida State University PhD Thesis.

Boissier, E. 1881. *Hemerocallis*. Flore Orientalis.

Bollinger, D. 1978. Two Basic Types of the Double-Flowered Hemerocallis. Hem. Jour. 32: #2 pp. 19-20

Botting, P. 1974. Germination of Diploid Daylily Seeds. Hem. Jour. 28: #2 pp. 45-49.

Brennan, J. R. 1991. The Control Mechanism: DNA & Chromosomes. Daylily Jour. 46: 393-397.

Brennan, J. R. 1992. The Chromosomes of *Hemerocallis*. Daylily Jour. 47: 73-77.

Brennan, J. R. 1994. Microscopic Location of Daylily Flower Pigments. Daylily Jour. 49: 207-213.

Bretschneider, E. 1962. Botanical Discoveries in China.

Brown, R. C. and Lemmon, B. E. 1991. Radial Microtubules Define Cytoplasmic Domains Following Faulty First Meiotic Division in Daylily. Amer. Jour. Bot. 78 *(Suppl.)*: 19-20.

Buck, W. Q. 1969. An "Injection" Method for Treating Hemerocallis Spikes with Colchicine. Hem. Jour. Yearbook 1969 pp. 42-43.

Burd, J. E. and Hart, M. B. 1979. Anatomy of the Double Daylily Bloom. Hem. Jour. 33: #1 pp. 79-81.

Chase, N. 1994. Triploids Are Fertile. Daylily Jour. 49: 37-42.

Chen, C. H. and Holden, D. J. 1972. Organogenesis in Daylily Callus. Proc. S. Dakota Acad. Sci. 51: 146-149.

Chen, C. N. and Golden-Kallemeyer, Y. C. 1979. *In vitro* Induction of Tetraploid Plants from Colchicine Treated Diploid Daylily Callus. Euphytica 28: 705-709.

Chung, M. G., Chung, H. G. and Kang, S. S. 1994. Distribution and Morphometric Analysis of *Hemerocallis hakunensis* and *H. thunbergii*. Korean Jour. Plt. Tax. 24: 17-32.

Chung, M. G. and Kang, S. S. 1994. Morphometric Analysis of the Genus Hemerocallis L. (Liliaceae) in Korea. Amer. Jour. Bot. 81 (Suppl.): 147-148.

Chung, M. G. and Kang, S. S. 1994. Hemerocallis hongdoensis (Liliaceae): A New Species from Korea. Novon 4: 94-97.

Claar, E. A. 1949. Daylily Report, 1948. Plt. Life 81: 45-49.

Coe, F. W. 1958. The Hemerocallis Species. Hem. Jour. 12: 152-156.

Corliss, P. G. 1950. Daylily Adaptability. Plt. Life 82: 123-124.

Corliss, P. G. 1951. Hemerocallis Comes of Age. Nat. Hort. Mag.: 146-153.

Corliss, P. G. 1968. Cultivars of Daylily. Amer. Hort. Mag. 47: 152-163.

Courtney, S. E., Rider, C. C. and Stead, A. D. 1994. Changes in Protein Ubiquitination and the Expression of Ubiquitin-encoding Transcripts in Daylily Petals During Floral Development and Senescence. Physiologia Plantarum 91: 196-204.

Creech, J. L. 1968. Exploring Daylilies in Japan. Amer. Hort. Mag. 47: 247-249.

Dark, S. O. S. 1932. Meiosis in Diploid and Triploid Hemerocallis. New Phytol. 31: 310-320.

Darrow, G. M. 1963. Hemerocallis aurantiaca littoria and Its Use in Breeding. Hem. Jour. 17: 23-25.

Daylily Handbook. A Special Issue on Hemerocallis. 1968. Amer. Hort. Mag. 272 pp.

Davis, B.A. 1954. Daylilies and How to Grow Them. Tupper and Love. 149 pp.

Deno, N. C. 1991. Seed Germination, Theory and Practice. Self-published. 96 pp.

Dress, W. J. 1955. Hemerocallis lilio-asphodelus, the Yellow Daylily. Baileya 3: 107-108.

Dunbar, C. 1984. Growing Daylilies in Containers. Daylily Jour. 38: 169-172.

Erhardt, W. 1992. Hemerocallis. Daylilies. Timber Press. 160 pp.

Fay, O. W. 1964. Report on Tetraploid Hemerocallis 1954-1964. Hem. Jour. Yearbook 1964. pp. 55-57.

Fischer, H. A. 1968. Daylilies in other Countries. Amer. Hort. Mag. 47: 250-254.

Flory, W. B. 1968. Daylilies in Landscaping and for Erosion Control. Amer. Hort. Mag. 47: 210-213.

Flory, W. B. 1968. Daylily Breeding in the North. Hem. Jour. 22: 19-26.

Flory, W. S. 1964. Chromosomes of Hemerocallis George Gilmer. Plt. Life 20: 48-49.

Flory, W. S. and Phillips, R. P. 1968. Chromosome Numbers in Hemerocallis washingtonia Static Dwarf Plants. Plt. Life 24: 84-86.

Foret, J. A. and Nelson, I. S. 1967. Propagation of Hemerocallis by Ramet Cuttage. Hem. Jour. 21: 44-49.

Fullmer, E. 1899. The Development of the Microsporangia and Microspores of Hemerocallis fulva. Bot. Gaz. 28: 81-88.

Gill, D. L. and Heald, C. M. 1968. Diseases of the Daylily. Amer. Hort. Mag. 47: 207-209.

Griesbach, R. A., Fay, O. W. and Horsfall, L. 1963. Induction of Polyploidy in Newly Germinated Hemerocallis Seedlings. Hem. Jour. 17: 70-75.

Griesbach, R. J. 1989. Selection of a Dwarf Hemerocallis Through Tissue Culture. Hort. Sci. 24: 1027-1028.

Griesbach, R. J. 1990. Genetic Engineering of Hemerocallis. Daylily Jour. 45: 278-281.

Griesbach, R. J. 1995. Flower Pigments within Hemerocallis fulva L. fm. fulva, fm. rosea, and fm. disticha. Hort Sci. 30: 353–354.

Grooms, A. O. 1971. Evolution of a Double Daylily. Hem. Jour. 25: #1 pp. 41-42.

Grovenstein, E. 1989-1994. That's a Good Question - column, general/scientific, Daylily Jour. 43: 390-391; 44: 21-25, 165-168, 229-233, 360-362; 43: 20-23, 138-145, 254-262, 355-356; 46: 35-41, 142-145, 252-256, 354-359; 47: 50-52, 150-155, 254-260, 346-354; 48: 50-55, 188-194, 268-275, 410-412; 49: 56-65, 190-196, 318-319, 404-411.

Grovenstein, E. 1993. Polytepalism/Variegated Foliage. Collection from column "That's a Good Question" booklet form. AHS.

Halinar, J. C. 1984. Blue Daylily—Is It Really So Simple? Daylily Jour. 38: 337-340.

Halinar, J. C. 1988. Classifying Foliage Types in Daylilies. Daylily Jour. 42: 48-50.

Halinar, J. C. 1988. Factors Affecting Fertility in Daylilies. Daylily Jour. 43: 401- 405.

Halinar, J. C. 1989. Diagnosing Fertility Problems in Daylilies—Part II. Daylily Jour. 44: 51-56.

Halinar, J. C. 1990. Breeding Methods for Daylilies. Daylily Jour. 45: 24-29.

Halinar, J. C. 1990. Polyploidy and Unreduced Gametes. Daylily Jour. 45: 339-346.

Hall, D. F. 1941. One Daylily I Like. Herbertia 8: 64-69.

Hamblin, S. 1957. Dwarf Daylilies. Hem. Jour. 11: #4 p. 22.

Hara, H. 1938. Hemerocallis coreana. Jour. Jap. Bot. 14: 520.

Hara, H. 1941. Hemerocallis vespertina. Jour. Jap. Bot. 17: 127-128.

Hart, M. B. 1979. Notes on Daylily Tolerance of Salt Water Used to Control Crown Rot. Hem. Jour. 33: #2 pp. 20-21.

Hava, W. C. 1960. Floral Pigment. Hem. Jour. 14: 101-102.

Hava, W. C. 1965. Floral Pigments of the Hemerocallis. Hem. Jour. 19: 46-49.

Hava, W. C., Esser, R. P., and Jenkins, W. R. 1962. Nematodes (Scientific Committee report) Hem. Jour. 16: #2 pp.15-19.

Heuser, C. W. and Apps, D. A. 1976. In Vitro Plantlet Formation from Flower Petal Explants of Hemerocallis cv Chipper Cherry. Can. Jour. Bot. 54: 616-618.

Hill, L. and N. 1991. Daylilies. The Perfect Perennial. Storey Comm., Inc.

Hisauchi, K. 1929. Botanical Notes From the Tochukew. Jour. Jap. Bot. 6: 113.

Holcomb, G. E. 1977. A Virus-Like Disease of the Daylily. Hem. Jour. 31: #3 pp. 13-14.

Hu, S-Y. 1964. Other Uses of Daylilies. Gdn. Jour. 223-228.

Hu, S-Y. 1968. An Early History of the Daylily. Amer. Hort. Mag. 47: 51-85.

Hu, S-Y. 1968. The Species of Hemerocallis. Amer. Hort. Mag. 47: 86-111.

Hu, S-Y. 1968. Uses of Daylily as Food and in Medicine. Amer. Hort. Mag. 47: 214-218.

Hu, S-Y. 1969. Exploration for New Daylilies in South Korea and Japan—June 10 to June 23, 1969. Hem. Jour. 23: 12-30.

Irish, N. 1972. Seed Treatment with Colchicine. Hem. Jour. 26: #1 pp. 15-19.

Kasha, M. 1977. On Inducing Fertility Through Polyploidy. Hem. Jour. 31: #2 p. 22.

Kasha, M. 1978. New Insights for the Amateur and Professional *Hemerocallis* Hybridizer. Hem. Jour. 32: 45-60.

Kasha, M. 1984. Hybridizing for a Blue Daylily—A Response. Daylily Jour. 38: 341-342.

Kasha, M., Bisset, K. E. and Sengupta, Pradeep K. 1984. Is the Blue Daylily Near? Daylily Jour. 36: #2 p.p. 68-80.

Kawano, S. 1961. On the Natural Hybrid Population of *Hemerocallis*. Can. J. Bot. 39: 667-681.

King, W. A. 1968. Breeding of Diploid Daylilies. Amer. Hort. Mag. 47: 164-166.

Kitchingman, R. M. 1983. A Survey of *Hemerocallis* Species. Brit. Hosta. Hem. Soc. Bull. 1: 28-39

Kitchingman, R. M. 1984. Preserving the *Hemerocallis*. Bull. Hardy Plt. Soc. 6: 123..

Kitchingman, R. M. 1985. A Survey of *Hemerocallis* Species, Part 1. Brit. Hosta. Hem. Soc. Bull. 1(3): 29-33; *Hemerocallis citrina*. 47: 168-170

Koidzuni, G. 1925. *Hemerocallis esculenta* Koidz nov. sp. Bot. Mag. Tokyo 39: 28.

Konar, R. N. and Stanley, R. G. 1969. Wall Softening Enzymes in the Gynoecium and Pollen of *Hemerocallis fulva*. Planta 84: 304-310.

Krikorian, A. D., Staicu, S. A. and Kann, R. P. 1981. Karyotype Analysis of a Daylily Clone Reared from Aseptically Cultured Tissues. Ann. Bot. 47: 121-131.

Krikorian, A. D., and Kann, R. P. 1979. Micropropagation of Daylilies Through Aseptic Culture Techniques: Its Basis, Status, Problems and Prospects. Hem. Jour. 33: #1 pp. 44-61.

Krikorian, A. D. and Kann, R. P. 1980. Mass Blooming of a Daylily Clone Reared from Cultured Tissues. Hem. Jour. 34: 35-38.

Lachman, W. H. 1972. Leaf Disorder of *Hemerocallis*. Hem. Jour. 26: #2 pp. 28-29.

Lachman, W. H. 1973. Potential Combining Abilities of Cultivar 'Lavender Parade' for Breeding *Hemerocallis* Hybrids. Hem. Jour. 26: #3 pp. 16-18.

Lambert, J. R. 1978. Some Reflections on Color and Value in Hybrid *Hemerocallis*. Hem. Jour. 32: #3 pp. 11-13.

Lange, N. E., Guerrero-Ruiz, C., Valpuesta, V. and Reid. M. S. 1993. Molecular Analysis of Petal Senescence in Daylily *Hemerocallis spp*. Plt. Physiol. 102 (Suppl.): 10.

Lange, N. E., Valpuesta, V., Guerrero, C., Botella, M. A., and Reid. M. S. 1994. Up-regulation of a MADS-box Gene Accompanies Daylily (Hemerocallis) Flower Senescence. Plt. Physiol. 105 (Suppl.): 42.

Makino, T. 1961. New Illustrated Flora of Japan. 836-837.

Mansfield-Jones, R. D. 1973. Disease and Insect Problems Affecting *Hemerocallis* in the South. Hem. Jour. 27: #3 pp 23-24.

Matsuoka, M. 1964. Wild *Hemerocallis* in Japan. Hem. Jour. 18: 38-40.

Matsuoka, M. 1970. Notes on *Hemerocallis dumortieri* Morren Variety *exaltata* (Stout) Kitamura on the Island of Tobishima. Japan. Hem. Jour. 24: 14-19.

Matsuoka, M. 1971. Spontaneous Occurrence of Triploid *Hemerocallis* in Japan. Jap. Jour. Breed. 21: 275-284.

Matsuoka, M. 1972. Cytological Studies on Hybrids Between Triploid and Diploid *Hemerocallis*. Jap. Jour. Breed. 22: 168-171.

Matsuoka, M., and Hotta, M. 1966. Classification of *Hemerocallis* in Japan and Its Vicinity. Acta Phyrotax. Geobot. 22: 25-38.

McEwen, C. 1974. Report on Presentation by Harold Harris (clonal treatment with colchicine). Hem. Jour. 28: #4 pp. 25-28

Melton, R., Kelly, J. and Whitwell, T. 1989. Physiological Response of Hosta, Daylily, and Yellow Nutsedge to Bentazon. Hort. Sci. 24: 1009-1010.

Meyer, M. M. 1976. Propagation of Daylilies by Tissue Culture. Hort. Sci. 11: 485- 487.

Meyer, M. M. 1979. Rapid Propogation of *Hemerocallis* by Tissue Culture. Hem. Jour. 33: #3 pp. 20-23.

Morrison, B. Y. 1928. The Yellow Day Lilies. USDA Circular No. 42: 1-14.

Munson, R. W. 1989. *Hemerocallis, The Daylily*. Timber Press Inc. 144 pp.

Nagle, J. S. 1991. A Comparison of the Physiology of Old and New Daylilies. Daylily Jour. 46: 174-179.

Nakai, T. 1932. *Hemerocallis japonica*. Bot. Mag. 46: 111-123.

Nakai, T. 1943. *Hemerocallis micrantha*. Jour. Jap. Bot. 19: 315.

Navain, P. 1979. Cytomixis in Pollen Mother Cells of *Hemerocallis* Linn. Curr. Sci. 48: 996-997.

Nesmith, E., Lester, M., Fischer, H. A., Craig, T. and Baker, S. H. 1960. Importance of the Species in Modern Breeding. Hem. Jour. 14: 87-88.

Noguchi, J. 1986. Geographical and Ecological Differentiation in the *Hemerocallis dumortierii* Complex with Special Reference to Its Karyology. Jour. Sci. Hiroshima U. 20: 29-123.

Noguchi, J., Tasaka, M. and Iwabuchi, M. 1992. The Historical Differentiation Process in *Hemerocallis middendorfii* Liliaceae of Japan Based on Restriction Site Variations of Chloroplast DNA. Amer. Jour. Bot. 79 (Suppl.): 156.

Norton, J. 1973. How to Cure Spring Sickness in Daylilies. Hem. Jour. 27: #2 pp. 22-29.

Norton, J. 1972. Some Basic Hemerocallis Genetics. Hem. Jour. 23: #2 pp. 29-39; #3, pp. 18-29. 24: #1 pp. 20-27. Also AHS mini-book collection.

Norton, J. B. S. 1945. *Hemerocallis* Through the Year. Nat. Hort. Mag. 197-199.

Peck, V. 1961. In Defense of Scientists. Hem. Jour. 15: 66-68.

Peck, V. 1964. Induction and Identification of Polyploidy in Hemerocallis. Hem. Jour. Yearbook 1964 pp. 57-61.

Peck, V. 1964. Tetraploid *Hemerocallis Breeding Results* for 1963. Hem. Jour. 18: 62-64.

Peck, V. 1973. Looking Back on Tetraploid Breeding. Hem. Jour. 27: #2 pp. 19-22.

Peck, V. 1988. Screening the Ploidy of a Colchicine Treated Plant of the Daylily Cultivar "Siloam Medallion." Daylily Jour. 43: 406-409.

Peck, V. 1989. The "Tet" Convention of '61 - I Was There. Daylily Jour. 44: 136-141.

Peck, V. and Arisumi, T. 1968. Tetraploid Daylilies. Amer. Hort. Mag. 47: 169-177.

Peck, V. and Peck, R. 1969. Breeding and Improvements in Tetraploid Daylilies. Hem. Jour. Yearbook 1969 pp. 33-39.

Petit, T. L. 1994. The Form of the Double Daylily. Daylily Jour. 49: 379-386.

Romine, J. 1983. Colchicine Treatment—A Simple Method. Daylily Jour. 37: 129-131.

Sanders, L. C. and Lord, E. M. 1989. Directed Movement of Latex Particles in the Gynoecia of Three Species of Flowering Plants. Jour. Cell Biol. 109: 325A.

Sanders, L. C. and Lord, E. M. 1989. Directed Movement of Latex Particles in the Gynoecia of Three Species of Flowering Plants. Science 243: 1606-1608.

Sato, S-I. 1984. A Cytochemical Study of the Embryo Sac Formation in *Hemerocallis middendorfii var. esculenta.* Jap. Jour. Gen. 60: 53-61.

Sato, S-I. 1985. Changes in the Distribution of Iron During Embryo Sac Development of *Hemerocallis middendorfii var. esculenta.* Jap. Jour. Gen. 61: 83-87.

Savage, R. H. 1972. Clonal Conversion Clinic at the Indianapolis Convention. Hem. Jour. 26: #4 pp. 17-24.

Saxton, S. 1977. Foliage Habits and Winter Injury of Daylilies. Hem. Jour. 31: 21-22.

Schabell, J. 1990–1995 (series "Historical Species") Daylily Jour. The Ancestor, 45: 159-160; Species Over Time and Space, 45: 282-284; Daylily - 5000 Years of Glory, 45: 348-352; *H. fulva* (L.) L. - Complex, Complex, 46: 42-44; *H. fulva* (L.) L. - Three Sisters, Rosea, 46: 163-165; Double variants of *H. fulva,* 46: 239-246; *H. fulva* (L.) L. - Complex, Complex. Lesser Known Variants; 46: 388-392; *H. citrina,* 47: 168-170; *H. dumortierii,* 47: 283-286; *H. middendorffii,* 48: 59-61; *H. lilioasphodelus,* 48: 174-177; *H. lilioasphodelus,* 48: 174-177; *H. thunbergii,* 48: 300-303; *H. aurantiaca.* The "Unspecies," 49: 96-101; *H. aurantiaca major.* The "Unspecies," 49: 224-228; *H. minor, H. multiflora, H. altissima,* 49: 310-316; *H. forrestii, H. nana, H. plicata, H. darrowiana, H. exaltata, H. tazaifu,* 49: 387-391; Historical Species, conclusion, 50: 48-53.

Sellers, V. 1979. Daylily Deaths. Hem. Jour. 33: #2. pp. 18-20.

Shull, J. M. 1940. Official Data Card for *Hemerocallis.* Herbertia 7: 98-102.

Shull, J. M. 1941. Some Daylily Problems. Herbertia 8: 36-39.

Shull, J. M. 1941. Initiation of Inflorescence in Daylilies. Herbertia 8: 126-129.

Shull, J. M. 1941. Cytology, Genetics and Breeding. Herbertia 8: 93-103.

Shull, J. M. 1943. Notes on Daylily Breeding. Herbertia 10: 129-130.

Sigel, C. W. 1985. The Daylily Species: Delicate and Enduring Flowers for the Perennial Garden. Daylily Jour. 39: 251-254.

Sigel, C. W. and Sigel, E. S. 1988. The Daylily Species: Recognition for Our Roots at the Judges' Table. Daylily Jour. 43: 410-412.

Smith, D. L. and Krikorian, A.D. 1991. Growth and Maintenance of an Embryogenic Cell Culture of Daylily (*Hemerocallis*) on Hormone-Free Medium. Ann. Bot. 67: 443-449.

Smith, F. F. 1960. Insects and Related Pests of Daylilies. Hem. Jour. Yearbook 1960 pp. 112-118.

Spencer, J. A. 1972. Collecephalus Hemerocallis, The Cause of Daylily Leaf-Streak: Morphology, Taxonomy, and Cultural Characteristics (Abstract). Daylily Jour. 26: #3 pp. 12-16.

Spencer, J. A. 1975. Current Known Diseases of the Daylily. Daylily Jour. 29: 23-25.

Spencer, J. A. 1985. Daylily Rot: A Reoccurring Nemesis. Daylily Jour. 39: 238-242.

Stamile, P. 1990. From Diploid to Tetraploid. Daylily Jour. 45: 242-249.

Sterrett, S. B., Brennan, J. R., Batdorf, L. R. and Spencer, R. D. 1994. Exploring Our Roots. Scientific Forum, AHS 1993 National Convention. Daylily Jour. 49: 198-205.

Stewart, A. 1958. *Hemerocallis.* Vascular Plants of the Lower Yangtze 512.

Stout, A. B. 1919. Seed Sterility in Plants that Reproduce Vegetatively. Jour. N.Y. Bot. Gdn. 20: 104-105.

Stout, A. B. 1921. Sterility and Fertility in Species of *Hemerocallis.* Torreya 21: 57-62.

Stout, A. B. 1925. New Daylilies. Jour. N.Y. Bot. Gdn. 26: 169-178.

Stout, A. B. 1926. The Capsules, Seeds and Seedlings of the Orange Day Lily. Jour. Hered. 17: 243-249.

Stout, A. B. 1929. The Fulvous Daylilies I. Jour. N.Y. Bot. Gdn. 30: 129-136.

Stout, A. B. 1929. The Fulvous Daylilies II. The Wild Fulvous Daylilies of the Orient. Jour. N.Y. Bot. Gdn. 30: 185-194.

Stout, A. B. 1929. *Hemerocallis aurantiaca.* Addisonia 14: 25-26.

Stout, A. B. 1929. *Hemerocallis flava.* Addisonia 14: 17-18.

Stout, A. B. 1929. *Hemerocallis minor.* Addisonia 14: 19-20.

Stout, A. B. 1929. *Hemerocallis fulva* clon maculata. Addisonia 14: 23-24.

Stout, A. B. 1929. *Hemerocallis dumortierii.* Addisonia 14: 27-28.

Stout, A. B. 1929. *Hemerocallis middendorffii.* Addisonia 14: 29-30.

Stout, A. B. 1929. *Hemerocallis multiflora.* Addisonia 14: 31-32.

Stout, A. B. 1930. The New Species *Hemerocallis multiflora.* Jour. N.Y. Bot. Gdn. 31: 34-39.

Stout, A. B. 1930. *Hemerocallis forrestii.* Addisonia 15: 1-2.

Stout, A. B. 1930. *Hemerocallis citrina.* Addisonia 15: 3-4.

Stout, A. B. 1930. *Hemerocallis fulva longituba.* Addisonia 15: 5-6.

Stout, A. B. 1930. *Hemerocallis fulva rosea.* Addisonia 15: 7-8.

Stout, A. B. 1930. *Hemerocallis* clon Luteola. Addisonia 15: 9-10.

Stout, A. B. 1930. *Hemerocallis* clon Gold Dust. Addisonia 15: 11-12.

Stout, A. B. 1930. *Hemerocallis* clon Mikado. Addisonia 15: 13.

Stout, A. B. 1930. *Hemerocallis* clon Wau-Bun. Addisonia 15: 15.

Stout, A. B. 1930. *Hemerocallis thunbergii.* Addisonia 15: 21-22.

Stout, A. B. 1930. Botanical Observations in Europe. Jour. N.Y. Bot. Gdn. 31: 261-264.

Stout, A. B. 1931. Notes on New Hybrid Daylilies. Jour. N.Y. Bot. Gdn. 32: 25-33.

Stout, A. B. 1932. The Bijou Daylily, of a New Small-Flowered Race. Jour. N.Y. Bot. Gdn. 33: 1-4.

Stout, A. B. 1932. The Soudan Daylily. Jour. N.Y. Bot. Gdn. 33: 104-105.

Stout, A. B. 1933. *Hemerocallis aurantiaca* and *Hemerocallis aurantiaca major.* New Flora and Silva 5: 187-192.

Stout, A. B. 1933. The Flowering Habits of Daylilies. Jour. N.Y. Bot. Gdn. 34: 25-32.

Stout, A. B. 1933. Gun-Jun or Gun-tsoy: A Food from the Flowers of Daylilies. Jour. N.Y. Bot. Gdn. 34: 97-100.

Stout, A. B. 1933. A Display Garden of Daylilies. Jour. N.Y. Bot. Gdn. 34: 135-139.

Stout, A. B. 1933. The New Daylily Taruga. Horticulture 27.

Stout, A. B. 1934. Dwarf Daylilies. Jour. N.Y. Bot. Gdn. 35: 1-8.

Stout, A. B. 1934. *Hemerocallis exaltata*. Addisonia 18: 37-38.

Stout, A. B. 1935. The Lemon Daylily (*Hemerocallis flava* L.): Its Origin and Status. Jour. N.Y. Bot. Gdn. 36: 61-68.

Stout, A. B. 1935. New Developments in Daylilies. Jour. N.Y. Bot. Gdn. 36: 205-216.

Stout, A. B. 1935. The Daylily on the Cover. Horticulture 13: 394.

Stout, A. B. 1937. Vegetative Propagation of Daylilies. Jour. N.Y. Bot. Gdn. 38: 13-17.

Stout, A. B. 1937. Two New Daylilies. Jour. N.Y. Bot. Gdn. 38: 60.

Stout, A. B. 1938. The New Boutonniere Daylily. Horticulture 380.

Stout, A. B. 1939. Three New Daylilies. Jour. N.Y. Bot. Gdn. 40: 32-35.

Stout, A. B. 1939. Daylilies With Rosy Pink Coloring. Horticulture 16: 226.

Stout, A. B. 1940. Foliage Habits of Daylilies. Herbertia 7: 157-165.

Stout, A. B. 1941. The Inflorescence in *Hemerocallis* I. Bull. Torrey Bot. Club 68: 305-316.

Stout, A. B. 1941. Report on Inter-Specific Hybridizations in *Hemerocallis*. Herbertia 8: 95-103.

Stout, A. B. 1941. Color Patterns in Daylilies. Jour. N.Y. Bot. Gdn. 42: 40-42.

Stout, A. B. 1942. Origin and Genetics of Some Classes of Red-Flowered Daylilies. Herbertia 9: 161-174.

Stout, A. B. 1942. *Hemerocallis altissima* Stout, *sp. nov.* Herbertia 9: 103-106.

Stout, A. B. 1942. Daylilies of Chinese Origin. Jour. N.Y. Bot. Gdn. 43: 237-243.

Stout, A. B. 1945. The Character and Genetics of Doubleness in the Flowers of Daylilies: The Para-Double Class. Herbertia 12: 113-123.

Stout, A. B. 1946. Introductions of Daylilies in 1946. Jour. N.Y. Bot. Gdn. 47: 77-82.

Stout, A. B. 1948. A New Race of Double-Flowered Daylilies. Jour. N.Y. Bot. Gdn. 49: 236-238.

Stout, A. B. 1949. Daylilies Being Introduced in 1949. Jour. N.Y. Bot. Gdn. 50: 36-39.

Stout, A. B. 1986. Daylilies. Sagapress, Inc. 145 pp.

Stoutmeyer, V. 1976. Alternative Methods of Propagation of Daylilies. Hem. Jour. 30: #4 pp. 20-22.

Stoutmeyer, V. 1976. New Advance in Container Plant Growing. Hem. Jour. 30: #4 pp. 22-23.

Stoutmeyer, V. 1976. Tissue Culture Propogation of Daylilies. Hem. Jour. 30: #2 pp. 10-12.

Stoutmeyer, V. 1977. Is Haploid Breeding of Daylilies Possible? Hem. Jour. 31: #1 pp. 20-21.

Takenoto, T. and Kusano, G. 1966. Studies on the Constituents of *Hemerocallis* I. Constituents of *Hemerocallis longituba*. Jour. Pharm. Soc. Japan. 86: 1116-1120.

Takenaka, Y. 1929. Karyological Studies in *Hemerocallis*. Cytologia 1: 76-83.

Tien, H. 1928. Untersuchen Uber die Sterilitatsursachen von *Hemerocallis fulva* und *citrina*. Planta 5: 784-308.

Traub, H. P. 1949. Colchicine Poisoning in Relation to *Hemerocallis* and Some Other Plants. Science 110: 686-687.

Traub, H. P. 1951. Colchicine-Induced *Hemerocallis* Polyploids and Their Breeding Behavior. Plt. Life 7: 83-116.

Traub, H. P. 1975. Saponins Absent in *Hemerocallis* L. Plt. Life 31: 106-107.

Uma, S., Gowda, J. V. N. and Joshi, S. 1994. Causes of Sterility in *Hemerocallis flava* L. Crop Res. (Hisar) 7: 491-493.

Unknown. *Hemerocallis* Tried at Wisley, 1929-1931. J. Royal Hort. Soc. 57: 107-113.

Unknown. 1962. Blue Blooding the Daylily. Hem. Jour. 16: 64-67.

Unknown. 1962. A *Hemerocallis* Variation. Am. Hort. Mag. 41: 238-239.

Vasak, V. 1971. *Hemerocallis Minor* at Home. Hem. Jour. 25: #2 pp. 37-40

Vaughn, W. P. 1968. Culture of Daylilies. Amer. Hort. Mag. 47: 197-200.

Vij, S. P., Shama, M. and Toor, I. S. 1978. Cytogenetical Investigations into Some Garden Ornamentals. Cytologia 43: 75-81.

Voth, P. D., Griesbach, R. A. and Yeager, J. R. 1968. Developmental Anatomy and Physiology in Daylily. Am. Hort. Mag. 47: 121-151.

Wallace, M. 1984. Scape Conversion. Daylily Jour. 38: 112-115.

Warner, L. 1969. Clonal Treatment with Colchicine or Colchicine Treatment of Adult Clones. Hem. Jour. Yearbook 1969 pp. 39-41.

Warner, M. 1968. Breeding of Miniature Daylilies. Am. Hort. Mag. 47: 167-168.

Webber, S. 1988. Daylily Encyclopedia. Webber Gardens.

Whatley, O. B. 1993. Identifying Converted Tets. Daylily Jour. 48: 199-201.

Whatley, O. B. 1993. Microscopic Identification. Daylily Jour. 48: 251-253.

Whatley, O. B. 1993. Safe Hybridizing. Daylily Jour. 48: 425-428.

Whatley, O. B. 1994. Pollen (dead or alive)? Daylily Jour. 49: 23-29.

Wollard, D. 1985. Apomixis Experiments Fail. Daylily Jour. 39: 171-173.

Wooten, J. 1975. Breeding Daylilies for Warm Regions. Proc. Fla. St. Hort. Soc. 88: 435.

Xiaobai, J. 1986. The Chromosomes of *Hemerocallis* (Liliaceae). Kew Bull. 41: 379-391.

Yang, H-Y. and Zhou, C. 1992. Experimental Plant Reproductive Biology and Reproductive Cell Manipulation in Higher Plants: Now and the Future. Amer. Jour. Bot. 79: 354-363.

Zadoo, S. H., Roy, R. P. and Khoshoo, T. N. 1976. Variation in Karyotype in *Hemerocallis*. La Cellule (Belguim) 71: 251-271.

Chapter 8
The Crystal Ball

The future is hidden even from the men who make it.
PAUL VALÉRY

Looking Over the Rainbow

ONE OF THE COMMON, perhaps essential characteristics of a serious hybridizer is the ability to see Utopia just around the bend. No matter that it never quite materializes, that the long-sought blue daylily is always somewhere just over the rainbow. Between those shades of red and blue are wonderful lavenders and purples. And if someone should dispute those color terms, there are surely exciting magentas and violets. The true hybridizer is not terminally put off. Some surprises must be reserved for next year's seedling crop. Perhaps only another hybridizer can explain the emotional highs and lows of the game. Over forty years ago, former board member Willard King, with his typical humorous perspective, described his introduction to hybridizing:

Some of my crosses took—some didn't. Anyway I was delighted with my new seed pods, which lost some of their glamour when I found out that they had to be planted a certain time in a certain way, then transplanted and re-transplanted. The day finally came when my first seedling bloomed and what a stinker it was, but to me it looked like the most beautiful flower I had ever seen. It confused me no end when no one else seemed to like it. But what a thrill! To know that you had helped to produce something new in the flower world—something which had never before or would ever again be just exactly like this one flower, even if it was a plug-ugly. That was all I needed. I couldn't wait for next year to come and I guess I made what seemed to me to be a thousand crosses which produced seeds, seeds and more seeds. I filled all the small cans and jars I could get my hands on but still I had seeds. I gave some away, found other small cans and jars and finally had this seed epidemic under control. This taught me to limit my crosses the next year and make them for some desired purpose. Little by little I learn the hard way, but brother you don't know you are living until you have made something new in the flower world come into bloom. Lordy, what a disease is this Hem Fever.—WILLARD KING

In the space of fifty years, hybridizers have brought astounding changes to the daylily. Color is one area of improvement. Scape height has been lowered dramatically. Petal width has increased to such a degree that modern *Hemerocallis* may be unrecognizable to the untrained eye.

If hybridizers have been criticized, with some justification, for prematurely naming their daylilies for tomorrow's colors, one can at least understand the excitement that led to all those "pinks" in the early Check Lists. The palette was limited to yellow, fulvous, and dull red. Colors were muddy. When *Hemerocallis fulva* var. 'rosea' appeared on the scene, it was indeed pink—by comparison. Today, color clarity has been achieved. Yes, dirty "dogs" still show up in the seedling patch, but unless a hybridizer has a particular affinity for them, they need not be selected.

A dramatic area of development during the last decade has been the emergence of *color patterns*. A step beyond the goal of color clarity, which occupied early breeders, new color patterns in daylilies have opened the door to dazzling effects. The first watermarked eyezones have spread to concentric rings of gray-blue. Some observers have commented that these eyes are the nearest thing to blue in "hemdom." Even more startling is the development of gold edging. When the first thin gold filigree showed around petals of pink and lavender blooms, gardeners were captivated. Now those threads have been exaggerated and combined with picotee and lace.

When the Society was formed, virtually no small-flowered or miniature daylilies were available in colors other than yellow. Growers now can choose from red, cream, purple, lavender, and pink.

Furthermore, those colors may come adorned with contrasting eyezones or patterns.

By and large, hybridizers have given gardeners what they asked for. A lesser body of designers would have become frustrated when the client reversed himself upon delivery and changed his order to tall and skinny! Not so, these indomitable hybridizers. Almost overnight, spiders began to emerge from heretofore hostile environments. One suspects that in the first rush of the 1980s, resurrection surpassed birth as a primary means of increasing the spider population. Nevertheless, industrious breeders set to work remedying inherently weak scapes and introducing tetraploidy to the spider form.

Spiders are not the only form to have benefited from the "retro" phenomenon of fashion. Not long ago, letters to the *Daylily Journal*'s popular column "That's a Good Question" by Erling Grovenstein latched onto the tendency for certain cultivars to produce extra petals. A great deal of discussion ensued over whether the trait was simply an incomplete form of doubling or something entirely different that bore watching. Granted, the occasional occurrence of this trait was nothing new in the history of daylilies, or other plants, for that matter. In fact, some growers considered it more abnormal than exciting. But once a *designer* gets an idea, couture happens. Enthusiastic supporters have now formed two round robins with the object of enhancing the form. Along with this newly appreciated form of beauty came the coined name, "polytepal."

The double daylily itself has enjoyed steady development in the last 50 years and, as a result, now is widely accepted as a desirable form in the garden. From the early *Hemerocallis fulva* "Kwanso" to the wide, full, symmetrical forms of today, double daylilies have come the distance. They are a credit to several dedicated hybridizers specializing in the form.

Not so evident in the gallery to follow is the generally improved blooming habit of daylilies. Many of the first hybrid daylilies suffered from a notoriously short bloom period. (Unfortunately, a few of today's introductions have this flaw as well, but it is far less prevalent now.) Genetic material likely to produce a longer bloom period was available for the taking in some of the species, but it was all yellow and small. At that time, hybridizers had other matters on their minds. Pink, for example. The widespread use of *Hemerocallis fulva* derivatives such as 'rosea' did nothing to further the everblooming habit. (*H. fulva* normally has 7 buds.) Eventually, with more hybridizers taking part and an expanding genetic pool, it became possible to introduce better bloom habit into all daylily classes. The quest for an "everblooming" daylily has produced higher bud count, better branching, repeat scapes, indeterminate or "bud-building" habit, and more attention to extended bloom or the ability to stay open for more than one day. It should be noted that these desirable traits are not likely to show up in a single package. Better late and early bloomers are providing another solution to an extended season.

As late as 1956, member-photographer Richard Montague made some interesting observations about the state of daylilies of his time:

> At the present stage of development many hems have uninteresting characteristics. The banal elongated oval, over-narrow segments, unrelieved straight edges, tiresome color similarity and color neutralization, lack of symmetry, gaping throats, segment bases too weak and spindly for true decorative value as the varied shapes developed, sweeping up and outward to produce the respective forms, the gamin-like projection of one petal (usually guarding the pistil) like a derisive tongue—all these detract from beauty.

Now Mr. Montague was not being hypercritical or unappreciative. He was simply being realistic in order to find the best approach to picture-taking, which he concluded lay in simplicity as opposed to ostentatious portraiture.

Nowadays we have a choice. Daylilies still lend themselves to graceful, three-quarter angled shots in the garden. But no longer are they "like human faces, best when not taken too seriously." Many of our newer daylilies can face a camera head-on without apology. The flaws that Richard Montague contrived to minimize in his viewfinder are no longer inevitable. Daylilies are available in great variety with good form, beautiful symmetry, ruffles and lace, clear colors, and wonderful new color patterns.

No, we still do not have a blue daylily, but it is just possible that the 100th Anniversary publication will feature one on its cover.

Progress is Now

OME 300 HYBRIDIZERS combine to register approximately 1,000 new daylilies in any given year. Not every registration represents an advance, but a steady overall improvement becomes obvious when looking backward fifty years.

What are hybridizers registering today? We asked them to send slides to illustrate their newest work.

We also required that those participating subsidize the cost of printing the following section. This requirement, unfortunately, eliminated many worthy new daylilies. However, it produced a more manageable sampling of outstanding work being done in the 1990s.

The AHS is proud of its hybridizers and their accomplishments.

❦ A LISTING OF HYBRIDIZERS WHOSE WORK IS PICTURED IN THIS CHAPTER ❧

KEY TO ABBREVIATIONS

Dip = diploid; Tet = tetraploid; Dbl = double; E = early; M = midseason; L = late; Re = recurrent; Dor. = dormant; Ev. = evergreen; Semi-ev. = semi-evergreen.

NOTE: Scape height and other measurements are as registered by the hybridizer. Cultural and climatic conditions may affect growth habit. Dates following hybridizer code names refer to date of registration.

8-1. FANCY FACE (Jack Carpenter) R. 1994, 5½ in. dia., 22 in. height, Dip, EMRe Ev.

8-2. CASTLE DOUBLE ROYALTY (Aileen Castlebury) R. 1995, 5¼ in. dia., 24 in. height, Dbl-Dip, M.

8-3. BRAZILIAN EMERALD (Victor Santa Lucia) R. 1992, 5¼ in. dia., 22 in. height, Tet, MRe, Dor.

8-4. GIVE ME EIGHT (Bill & Joyce Reinke) R. 1993, 8 in. dia., 48 in. height, Dip, Semi-ev. A "polytepal" form.

8-6. BIG BOO (Ra Hansen) R. 1994, 6½ in. dia., 28 in. height, Dip, EMRe, Semi-ev.

8-5. YANKEE TRADITION (Victor Santa Lucia) R. 1993, 5 in. dia., 28 in. height, Tet, MRE, Dor.

8-7. CALGORY STAMPEDE (Ra Hansen) R. 1994, 5 in. dia., 22 in. height, Tet, MLaRe, Semi-ev.

8-8. SMUGGLER'S GOLD (Charles E. Branch) R. 1991, 6 in. dia., 24 in. height, Tet, M, Dor.

8-10. *YABBA DABBA DOO (Ra Hansen) R. 1993, 10 in. dia., 30 in. height, Spider-Variant, LaRe, Semi-ev.*

8-9. *SILOAM PEONY DISPLAY (Pauline Henry) R. 1991, 6 in dia., 18 in. height, Dbl-Dip, M, Dor.*

8-11. *MISTER LUCKY (Van M. Sellers) R. 1995, 3¾ in. dia., 24 in. height, Tet, EMRe, Ev. (transfer of name)*

8-12. *MASKED PHANTOM (Van M. Sellers) R. 1995, 5 in. dia., 24 in. height, Tet, EM-M, Ev. (transfer of name)*

8-13. *RUFFLES AND RAINBOWS (Darrel Apps)*
R. 1995, 6 in. dia., 20 in. height, Dip, M, Ev.

8-14. *SMOKY MOUNTAIN BELL (Lucille Guidry)*
R. 1992, 5½ in. dia., 25 in. height, Dip, ERe, Ev.

8-15. *PYROMANIAC (Davis Guidry) R. 1993,*
5 in. dia., 22 in. height, Dbl-Dip, ERe, Ev.

8-16. *MAGNIFICENT RAINBOW (Patrick M. Stamile)*
R. 1995, 6 in. dia., 17 in. height, Tet, LaRe, Dor.

8-17. *SILOAM GLORYLAND (Pauline Henry) R. 1992*
6 in. dia., 24 in. height, Dip, M, Dor.

8-18. *SILOAM OLIN FRAZIER (Pauline Henry)*
R. 1990, 5¼ in. dia., 22 in. height, Dbl-Dip, E, Dor.

8-19. *WINGS OF PEACE (Bob Love) R. 1992, 7 in. dia.,*
34 in. height, Tet, MRe, Dor.

8-20. *BREAKFAST BLUSH (Bob Love) R. 1992, 5 in. dia.,*
24 in. height, Tet, MRe, Dor.

8-21. *GLADYS CAMPBELL (Ted L. Petit) R. 1994,*
5½ in. dia., 19 in. height, Dbl-Tet, M, Ev.

8-22. *FORBIDDEN DESIRES (Ted L. Petit) R. 1995, 6 in. dia.,*
19 in. height, Tet, M, Semi-ev.

8-23. KINGS AND VAGABONDS (Ted L. Petit)
R. 1994, 6 in. dia., 22 in. height, Tet, M, Ev.

8-24. SUPER MOM (Ken Durio) R. 1991
6 in. dia., 20 in. height, Tet, EMRe, Ev.

8-25. CASTLE SUGAR CANDY (Aileen Castlebury)
R. 1994, 4½ in. dia., 27 in. height, Tet, MRe, Semi-ev.

8-26. COMING MOTHER (David A. Riseman) R. 1994,
5 in. dia., 24 in. height, Tet, EMRe, Dor.

8-27. RUSSELL RISEMAN (David A. Riseman) R. 1994,
7 in. dia., 26 in. height, Tet, EM, Dor.

8-28. LUCKY EYE (David A. Riseman) R. 1994, 3 in. dia.,
14 in. height, Dip, M, Dor.

MORNING BY MORNING (Charles & Linda Applegate)
R. 1994, 4½ in. dia., 28 in. height, Dbl, E, Semi-ev.

8-30. SOUTHERN FRIENDS (David A. Riseman) R. 1995,
5½ in. dia., 24 in. height, Tet, EM, Ev.

8-32. HUSH LITTLE BABY (Sarah Sikes) R. 1992, 5 in.
dia., 22 in. height, Dip, MLaRe, Dor.

8-31. SYDNEY EDDISON (Sarah Sikes) R. 1994, 5½ in.
dia., 25 in. height, Dip, MRe, Dor.

8-33. DESIGNER GOLD (Sarah Sikes) R. 1995, 5½ in.
dia., 32 in. height, Tet, MRe, Dor.

8-34. MAE WEST (Judith Weston) R. 1990, 7¼ in. dia., 20 in.
height, Dip, MLa, Semi-ev.

8-35. SLAM DUNK (*Judith Weston*) *R. 1995, 4¾ in. dia., 24 in. height, Tet, M, Ev.*

8-36. MARY ANN SMITH (*R. W. Munson, Jr.*) *R. 1993, 4½ in. dia., 24 in. height, Tet, MRe, Semi-ev.*

8-37. PARIS SIDEWALK CAFE (*R.W. Munson, Jr.*) *R. 1995, 5 in. dia., 24 in. height, Tet, MRe, Ev.*

8-38. TANGLEWOOD (*Betty Hudson*) *R. 1993, 5 in. dia., 20 in. height, Dbl-Tet, EM, Ev.*

8-40. SNOWY RIVER *(Ken Durio) R. 1992, 6½ in. dia., 28 in. height, Tet, EMRe, Ev.*

8-39. GRECIAN SANDS *(Betty Hudson) R. 1993, 6 in. dia., 34 in. height, Dbl-Tet, EMRe, Ev.*

8-41. AZURE VIOLETS *(Jean Duncan) R. 1995, 5¼ in. dia., 29 in. height, Tet, ERe, Ev.*

8-42. CRESTED GOLD SURF *(Jean Duncan) R. 1995, 5 in. dia., 26 in. height, Tet, EMRe, Ev.*

8-43. *CALLIE KAISER (Jean Duncan) R. 1995, 5 in. dia.,*
39 in. height, Tet, ERe, Ev.

8-44. *BROADWAY FLASH (Arthur Blodgett) R. 1993,*
6 in. dia., 30 in. height, Tet, MLa, Dor.

8-45. *TIVOLI NIGHTINGALE (Jean Duncan) R. 1995,*
5 in. dia., 20 height, Tet, MRe, Ev.

8-46. *TOTALLY AWESOME (S. Glenn Ward) R. 1993,*
7 in. dia., 28 in. height, Dbl-Dip, EMRe, Ev.

8-47. JIM McKINNEY *(Clarence J. Crochet)* R. 1994, 6 in. dia., 24 in. height, Tet, EMRe, Semi-ev.

8-48. JOIE DE VIVRE *(Lee E. Gates)* R. 1993, 6 in. dia., 22 in. height, Dip, ERe, Ev.

8-49. CHOCTAW BRIDE *(Lee E. Gates)* R. 1994, 6 in. dia., 26 in. height, Dip, ERe, Ev.

8-50. KING KAHUNA *(Clarence J. Crochet)* R. 1994, 6½ in. dia., 22 in. height, Dbl-Dip, EMRe, Semi-ev.

8-51. ALMOST INNOCENT (Lee E. Gates) R. 1994, 6 in. dia., 24 in. height, Dip, ERe, Semi-ev.

8-52. IN THE NAVY (Elizabeth Hudson Salter) R. 1993, 3 in. dia., 18 in. height, Dip, MRe, Semi-ev.

8-53. MARY ETHEL ANDERSON (Elizabeth H. Salter) R. 1995, 2½ in. dia., 18 in. height, Dip, MLaRe, Semi-ev.

8-54. UPPERMOST EDGE (Morton Morss) R. 1994, 5 in. dia., 21 in. height, Tet, MRe, Semi-ev.

8-55. *BARBARA DITTMER (Morton Morss) R. 1994, 3 ¾ in. dia., 24 in. height, Tet, ERe, Semi-ev.*

8-56. *BORDER MUSIC (Jeff Salter) R. 1995, 6 in. dia., 26 in. height, Tet, MRe, Semi-ev.*

8-57. *TOUCHED BY MAGIC (Jeff Salter) R. 1995, 5 in. dia., 26 in. height, Tet, MRe, Ev.*

8-58. *JEAN HIGH (David Kirchhoff) R. 1994, 6 in. dia., 25 in. height, Dbl, EMRe, Semi-ev.*

8-59. MOUNTAIN ALMOND (Oliver Billingslea)
R. 1991, 6 in. dia., 21 in. height, Dip, M, Semi-ev.

8-60. PEGGY TURMAN (David Kirchhoff) R. 1994, 6¾ in.
dia., 26 in. height, Dbl, MRe, Ev.

8-61. CHARLOTTE DEVILLIER (Ken Durio)
R. 1993, 6½ in. dia., 25 in. height, Tet, EMRe, Ev.

8-62. DE COLORES (John J. Temple) R. 1992, 8½ in. dia.,
28 in. height, Spider, ERe, Ev.

Concerns of Tomorrow

LMOST NO ONE DISPUTES the overt improvements made to daylilies in the last fifty years. If there is a cloud on the horizon, it falls below the line of view. Some claim that it does not exist at all, at least as an inherent part of the plant. Others insist that we have grave problems with

ROT!

Several years ago when growers picked up what seemed to be a trend for certain plants to succumb to a mysterious crown rot condition—particularly prevalent in the South—the AHS undertook to sponsor a study in Mississippi. No conclusive evidence came from that study, but several recommendations were made with regard to cultural precautions. Is there a genetic problem? A substantial number of highly respected hybridizers think so. One such concern was acknowledged by W. B. MacMillan as recorded by Clarence Crochet in V. 40, No. 2 of the *Daylily Journal:*

> After the death of Miss Spalding, Mr. Mac found a medium-sized, short-scaped, ruffled greenish yellow of extreme beauty in the seedling patch. He was so impressed that he named it EDNA SPALDING MEMORIAL. It represented a great leap forward in hybridizing; it was a green-yellow of rare refinement. Even though it presented some difficulty in transplanting, he introduced it for $100, fulfilling a long-held opinion that one day he would be the hybridizer of a daylily worth that much money. And it was a great deal of money in 1968! So distinctive was EDNA SPALDING MEMORIAL that hybridizers eagerly paid the amount to use it in their hybridizing programs.
>
> But there was trouble in paradise. A number of knowledgeable growers and hybridizers had perceived that some of his plants, as beautifully flowered as they were, had a serious fault—this fault was the tendency of "dying without cause" that had somehow crept into his bloodline. For example, he produced a gorgeous pink and decided that it would be the one flower to surpass all others as a breeder. Consequently, he loaded it with about 20 seed pods. However, before the seeds could ripen, the plant just rotted and died. Since it was the only plant of that particular pink, that dream was shattered.
>
> On another occasion, he produced a cream seedling that was as fine as any, so far it was ahead of its time. He was to sell it for $100 per fan. All fans that had been lined out for spring sale promptly died. That was that. Consequently, Mr. Mac destroyed all seeds and seedlings related to the cream seedling.
>
> After these setbacks, he destroyed other daylilies that he suspected had carried the hereditary susceptibility to "dying without cause."

During his 1991 interview with the regional vice presidents, Steve Moldovan of Ohio expressed strong opinions on the subject of rot:

> There are daylilies today that do rot. I have not had the rot problem in my garden. Only when I get them from the Deep South do I have rot. I've never had rot per se in great numbers in my garden.
>
> As a breeder, I could easily say that I could breed that rot out. That's a bunch of baloney. It failed with bearded iris. We breeders have to be aware of this problem and not use varieties that rot. I don't care how pretty they are. Do not use them because we will carry that gene. . . .
>
> There's a rotting gene out there. It seems the lethal gene for rot is connected with beauty. It's Mother Nature's way! We have to be careful. The breeder has to be the one to control this. If we neglect this and forget about it and say it's not going to happen in my line, we're fooling ourselves. We'll have a Society that will have to have seminars on fungicides and rotting. . . .
>
> The future of our favorite flower is in jeopardy. Right now. Today. The crosses that we're making today can determine that future.

No less eminent breeder than R. W. Munson, Jr. wrote at length of the problem in the preface to his 1989 book, *Hemerocallis, the Daylily:*

> . . . Over the past 25–30 years the daylily has become greatly refined and can now certainly be described as unique, beautiful, and varied. But regrettably it is not

as dependable as it once was and is indeed beginning to be fraught with infirmities, such as crown rot, the yellows, spring sickness, as well as a developing susceptibility to insects it never had in the early years. . . .

With awareness, can solutions be far behind? Hybridizers have shown great resourcefulness in solving problems of the past, and it does not seem unreasonable to expect that they will be successful in obliterating this dark cloud.

OTHER UNDESIRABLES

If the South has been a breeding ground for rot, the North may claim "spring sickness" as its own special nemesis. Both ill-defined and oft-disputed, it has never been collectively identified. Individual members have described it so variously as to give rise to the suspicion that we are dealing with more than one condition.

Daylilies are still susceptible to aphids, thrips, and red spider. Some growers contend the problem is worse now than fifty years ago. This author suggests that we simply have more daylilies now and grow them in circumstances that invite more bad bugs. No hard data exist to support either theory. It is encouraging to see gardeners in controlled areas having success growing daylilies without pesticides. The pest and insect problem eventually may be solved by genetic engineering. It is happening with other plants; why not daylilies?

THE POPULATION EXPLOSION

As far back as the first *Hemerocallis Check List*, Registrars Hamilton P. Traub and Harry Tuggle were predicting death by drowning in the tidal wave of registrations. It hasn't happened yet, perhaps only because we have learned to swim. Suggestions have been made for stemming the tide. Some would raise the registration fee. Others favor eliminating names no longer in commerce. A few would have AHS be more selective in the names and/or daylilies it accepts for registration.

While recognizing the potentially finite nature of our recording system in its current format, the AHS has never attempted to play the heavy regulatory hand as International Registry for *Hemerocallis*. The Society wants to *encourage*, not discourage registration. This long-standing policy is one of the reasons AHS has enjoyed remarkable cooperation from its hybridizers. The process is not so formidable that they are tempted to bypass it. Those 38,000 names may be a handful to manage, but at least they are corralled. Under the system which has worked well these fifty years, the burden of responsibility is on the hybridizers. They are called upon to be as discriminating as possible.

THE ROOT OF ALL EVIL

As the daylily has grown in popularity during the last decade, the AHS has begun to attract more members with an avaricious gleam in the eye. People who know little about daylilies and less about selling are frenetically doing both. Peripheral "services" have sprung up all over the country. New hybridizers are unknowingly registering daylilies that were surpassed 20 years ago.

Exaggerated claims for specific cultivars and for the genus itself have spread beyond the circulation of our own members (who know how to read and discount such excesses). The daylily is a wonderful plant, but it is not a panacea for every landscaping or environmental condition. To exploit it in this manner will eventually bring harm to both the daylily and the Society. Members can help by educating the general gardening public to the true value of growing daylilies. After all, it is our affair—our Fifty-Year Affair.

HANGING CREPE AND OTHER PERILOUS PLEASURES

Will the dark clouds come to pass? Or will the optimists prevail? Crafty seers don't look into the crystal ball and rashly enter their findings into a word processor as we have done here. Wisely, they mumble their jumbo.

Member George Gilmer proved his original premise when over thirty years ago he began with, "It is always hazardous to predict without a good crystal ball" [Stop right there, George, while you're ahead!], then continued recklessly: "but from what I have seen I fully believe that inside of three years the great majority of active breeders will be using tetraploid stock almost exclusively." (Hem. J., V.17, No. 3, p.40)

Chapter 9

The Last Laugh

You might as well laugh at yourself once in a while—
everyone else does.
EVAN ESAR

Steve Baldwin's "Hem-antics"

ROBERT BURNS must have had the *Hemerocallis* addict in mind when he penned these lines:

O wad some Pow'r the giftie gie us
To see oursels as others see us!
It wad frae mony a blunder free us,
And foolish notion:
What airs in dress an' gait wad lea'e us,
And ev'n devotion!

Popular garden writer Frederick McGourty made no bones about it: "My idea of purgatory is to sit next to a hemerocallis collector on a bus on the Long Island Expressway late on a Friday afternoon during a heat wave when the bus breaks down."

For several years, AHS member and artist Steve Baldwin of North Carolina has been rendering his impressions of daylily people in a series of cartoons he calls "Hem-antics." Several have appeared in the AHS Region 15 Newsletter, the *Hemalina*. Most intense daylily growers will recognize themselves in at least a few panels. Otherwise, the characters to follow are purely fictitious and any resemblance to actual persons, living or dead, is purely coincidental.

*"And he's missing **this** to play golf—I'll never understand people..."*

A tribute to hybridizers . . .

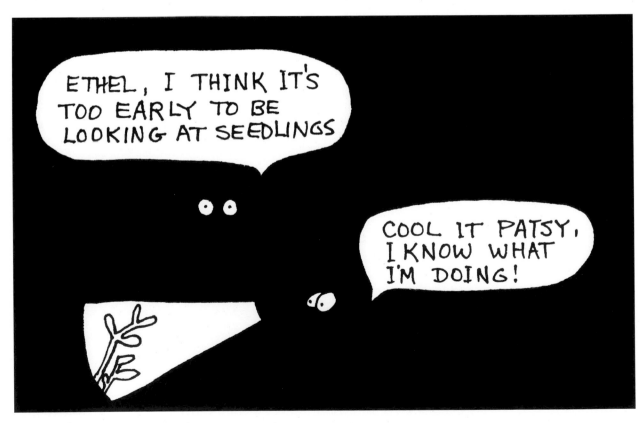

Secret formulas . . .

What a selection . . .

Mail orders . . .

Through the eyes of . . .

9-1. *Steve Baldwin.*
(photo by Harvey Horne)

Hem-antics

Daylily shows . . .

Illustrations

Sources

Primary sources used in the preparation of this book were AHS Yearbooks, Journals, Newsletters (regional and national), Hemerocallis Check Lists, and Judges' Handbooks. Due to the mass of volumes consulted, specific references are not given here. Unless otherwise cited within the text, extractions were taken from AHS publications. Other sources are credited at the point of entry or with the Acknowledgments.

Information on Shenandoah and its radio stations came from Jane & Michael Stern, "Neighboring," *The New Yorker*, April 1991; and from the Shenandoah Historical Society. The author also was privileged to hear about Shenandoah, past and present, from its friendly residents during an extended visit in 1994.

Key: Hemerocallis cultivars are entered in upper case to correspond with the system used in most AHS literature. Illustrations are not included here. (See list of Illustrations preceding subject index.) Page references in bold face denote substantive entries.